THEMATIC UNIT
Owls

Written by Fran Van Vorst

PARENT-TEACHER COLLECTION

Teacher Created Materials, Inc.
6421 Industry Way
Westminster, CA 92683
www.teachercreated.com
©1999 Teacher Created Materials, Inc.
Reprinted, 2000
Made in U.S.A.
ISBN-1-57690-375-3

Edited by
Janet Hale, M.S. Ed.

Illustrated by
Ken Tunell

Cover Art by
Cheri Macoubrie Wilson

Table of Contents

Introduction

Owls is a captivating, comprehensive, 80-page thematic unit designed to immerse children in writing, poetry, language arts, science, math, social studies, music, art, drama, and life skills. The literature and activities used in this thematic unit have been selected to help children gain a better understanding about owls. In addition, children will experience working cooperatively, being considerate of others, and taking into consideration other points of view. A variety of teaching strategies such as cooperative learning, hands-on experience, and child-centered assessment are integrated into the unit.

This thematic unit includes the following:

- ❏ **literature selections**—summaries of two children's books with related lessons (complete with reproducible pages) that cross the curriculum

- ❏ **poetry**—suggested selections and lessons enabling children to write and publish their own work

- ❏ **choral expression**—suggestions to encourage children to participate expressively in groups

- ❏ **planning guides**—suggestions for sequencing lessons each day of the unit

- ❏ **writing ideas**—daily suggestions as well as writing activities that reach across the curriculum

- ❏ **research topics**—ideas, to develop the ability to organize and report on subjects

- ❏ **bulletin board ideas**—suggestions and plans for child-created and/or interactive displays

- ❏ **comparing and contrasting**—activites to encourage children to develop critical evaluation

- ❏ **surveys and graphing**—exercises extending the theme mathematically to visualize personal thoughts and feelings

- ❏ **curriculum connections**—variety of activites in language arts, math, science, social studies, art, choral expression, drama, and life skills

- ❏ **culminating activities**—activities that require children to synthesize their learning and produce a product or engage in an activity that can be shared with others

- ❏ **a bibliography**—suggestions for additional fiction and nonfiction books on the theme, as well as Web sites and other helpful resources.

> To keep this valuable resource intact so that it can be used year after year, you may wish to punch holes in the pages and store them in a three-ring binder.

Introduction *(cont.)*

Why a Balanced Approach?

The strength of a balanced language approach is that it involves children in using all modes of communication—reading, writing, listening, illustrating, and doing. Communication skills are interconnected and integrated into lessons that emphasize the whole of language. Implicit in this approach is our knowledge that every whole—including individual words—is composed of parts, and directed study of those parts can help a student master the whole. Experience and research tell us that regular attention to phonics, other word attack skills, spelling, etc., develops reading mastery, thereby fulfilling the unity of the whole language experience. The child is thus led to read, write, spell, speak, and listen confidently in response to a literature experience introduced by the teacher. In these ways, language skills grow rapidly, stimulated by direct practice, involvement, and interest in the topic.

Why Thematic Planning?

One very useful tool for implementing an integrated whole language program is thematic planning. By choosing a theme with correlating literature selections for a unity of study, a teacher can plan activities throughout the day that lead to a cohesive, in-depth study of the topic. Children will be practicing and applying their skill in meaningful contexts. Consequently, they will tend to learn and retain more. Both teachers and children will be freed from a day that is broken into unrelated segments of isolated drill and practice.

Why Cooperative Learning?

Besides academic skills and content, children need to learn social skills. No longer can this area of development be neglected or be taken for granted. Children must learn to work cooperatively in order to function in modern society. Group activities should be a regular part of a school day, and teachers should consciously include social objectives as well as academic objectives in their planning. For example, a group working together to write a report may need to select a leader. The teacher should make it clear to the children about the leader's position and monitor the leader-follower group interaction just as he/she would the basic goals of the project.

Why Big Books?

An excellent cooperative language activity is the production of big books. Groups of children, or the entire class, can apply their language skills, content, knowledge, and creativity to produce a big book that can become a part of the classroom library. These created books may then be read and reread during free-reading sessions. Big books make excellent culminating projects for sharing beyond the classroom with parents, librarians, other classes, etc.

Why Journals?

Each day your children should have the opportunity to write in a journal. They may respond to a book read or an event in history, write about a personal experience, or answer a general "question of the day" posed by the teacher. Journals also provide an excellent means of documenting a child's writing progress.

Owl Moon

by Jane Yolen

Summary

The award-winning book Owl Moon *is a delightful story about a young child who is excited and honored to be old enough to go owling. Dressed warmly and not making a sound, he and Pa walk into the woods. The snow crunches under their feet, and their footprints and shadows can be seen behind them. Pa calls for the Great Horned owl. After no reply, they walk deeper into the woods. This time when Pa calls out, an echo returns. It is not just an ordinary echo. It is the majestic echo of a Great Horned owl. The young boy and his pa return home, pleased that their owling adventure was successful—and a special memory they could share forever.*

The outline below is a suggested plan for using the various activities that are presented in this unit. You should adapt these ideas to fit your own classroom situation.

Sample Plan

Lesson 1

- Brainstorm descriptive words about owls (page 6, Setting the Stage, #3).
- Begin a KWL chart (page 8).
- Read and discuss *Owl Moon*.
- Complete Story Mapping (page 7, #1).
- Make hooty owls for your bulletin board display (page 70).

Lesson 2

- Review *Owl Moon*.
- Add learned facts to the KWL Chart.
- Label Parts of an Owl (page 7, #6).
- Have lunch with Owly (page 30).
- Introduce owl symmetry (page 42, Lesson 1).
- Create pine cone hooty owls (page 52).

Lesson 3

- Recall details of *Owl Moon*.
- Put sentence strips in order (pages 10 and 11) and make a big book (page 12).
- Play an owl number families math game (page 48).
- Weave owl place mats (page 53).

- Explore an owl's food chain (page 74).
- Make and eat Mouse Salad for an Owl (page 63).

Lesson 4

- Create "The Important Things About Owls" Booklet (page 7, #4).
- Create owl cinquain poems (page 27).
- Decorate the poems with Thumbprint owls (page 52).
- Complete the Owl Crossword Puzzle (page 31).
- Read the Whooo? Choral Poem while using the flannelboard drama panels (page 7, #8).

Lesson 5

- Complete When You Go Owling...(page 7, #3).
- Review *Owl Moon*.
- Solve Spotty Owl's problems (page 49).
- Create owl silhouettes (page 55).
- Compare owl and songbird skeletons (page 7, #7).

Overview of Activities

Setting the Stage

1. Prepare the classroom for the owls theme by setting up an owls learning center and bulletin board (page 70).

2. As a beginning to the theme, find out what your children already know about owls and what they would like to know by preparing a KWL chart (page 8). The children will give their ideas and you will record what they know and what they want to know. If some of the children's facts are incorrect, still record them on the chart. As study of the theme progresses, the children can reassess their knowledge of owls and correct the chart. The facts and questions generated can be used to plan activities for the unit.

3. Put up chart paper and ask the children to participate in offering descriptive words and phrases pertaining to owls. The descriptive words will be valuable if you choose to have the children make daily journal writing entries (page 24).

4. Lead a discussion about where owls like to live (barns, hollows of trees, etc.) and when owls like to hunt for food (nighttime). The Food Chain Chart (page 74) will help the children understand the valuable role owls play in the environment. You may want to enlarge the Food Chain Chart. This can be done by using the enlarging features on a copying machine or by making an overhead transparency and using an overhead projector.

5. Prepare the owl poems, chant, and songs (pages 23 and 56) on chart paper to be on display in the room. Encourage the children to memorize a poem or song.

6. The Owl Reference Charts (pages 72 and 73) are designed to be a resource for you and your children when searching for quick facts on owls. The most common owls are featured on these charts. If the children need to search for more in-depth information you will need to provide detailed reference books such as those suggested in the bibliography (pages 79 and 80). A practice page for learning more about owls can be found on page 35.

Enjoying the Book

1. Show the cover of *Owl Moon* and ask the children to predict what the events of the story might be. Their input will help to build anticipation for the reading of the story.

2. After reading the first page, show the children the illustration and discuss the main characters of the story. Draw the children's attention to the color tones and how they create a particular atmosphere. Build excitement about what might happen next.

3. After the story is read, discuss the concept of "owling" and explain that there are people who enjoy going out in the forest to observe owls. Many naturalists record the habits of owls while they are in the woods studying them. If possible, plan a nighttime field trip into the woods to observe owls. (**Note:** Be certain to take lots of parental assistance, binoculars, cameras, and wear warm clothing.)

Overview of Activities (cont.)

Extending the Book

1. The story mapping activity (page 9) will help review *Owl Moon* in a concise manner. In this activity the children are asked to retell the story using four pictures and to explain each picture by writing a sentence or two on the provided lines. The children will then cut out the boxes and assemble the boxes in order (1–4) to form a minibook. Staple the book along the left-side edge to form the minibook's spine.

2. The sentence strips (pages 10 and 11) permit your children to recall the main points of the story. The children can work individually or cooperatively. The strips are to be cut out and put in order on a separate sheet of paper or displayed in a pocket chart. The strips can also be used as the text for a big book. As an extension, have the children work cooperatively to make a big book. The making of a big book is explained on page 12. You may wish to display the completed big book in your room or in the library.

3. When You Go Owling...(page 13) allows the children to express what they would do if they were the child in the story and had a chance to go owling.

4. Make a "The Important Things About Owls" booklet, following the pattern from *The Important Book* by Margaret Wise Brown (see page 79). The book's pattern is described on page 25. The booklet may be made in the shape of an owl (page 29). On each page of the booklet there should be one important fact about owls. The last page of the booklet should textually describe the one thing the children think is the most important thing about owls. Stack the completed booklet pages and staple them together along the left side to form the book's spine.

5. Read a different fiction or nonfiction book about owls to your children each day (see pages 79 and 80). Encourage your children to read about owls at home, as well.

6. A labeled diagram of an owl can be found on page 75. This chart will help your children with the science activity, Parts of an Owl (page 33), where the children fill in their own diagrams by using the word bank provided.

7. Conduct an observation activity comparing an owl's and a songbird's skeletons (page 34). The children begin by studying the illustrations of the two bird skeletons. Create a Venn diagram: one circle for the characteristics of the owl, one circle for the characteristics of another bird species, and the overlapping section for what is common about both types of birds.

   Resources for owl information can be found on the Owl Reference Charts (pages 72 and 73) or from reference materials listed on pages 79 and 80. Reference materials on songbirds can be obtained from your school or community library.

8. Enjoy reading the choral poem Whooo? (page 57) as well as using the Five Wise Owls flannel-board drama panels (pages 58–62).

KWL Chart

A KWL chart is a visual aid designed to help children classify their thoughts. The chart has three sections: prior knowledge (**K**now), curiosity knowledge (**W**ant to Know), and acquired knowledge (**L**earned). Create the chart on chart paper or a section of a chalkboard. Have the children tell you what they already know about owls and list that knowledge in the first section. Next have the children tell what they would like to know about owls and list their questions in the second section of the chart. The last section will be filled in as the unit progresses and the children discover new facts. The chart should be on display during the entire theme. When a Learned fact is discovered that answers a question in the Want to Know section, indicate this by placing a sticker or colored star beside the question in the second section and print the learned knowledge in the third section (using a corresponding sticker or colored star next to the just-written fact).

KWL charts serve as an excellent child-centered resource for providing authentic assessment. KWL charts can also be used as a source of information for children as they write stories, illustrate child-created books, or review unit facts.

Know	Want to Know	Learned
Owls have sharp talons. Owls come in all sizes. Owls have many colors.	Do owls have babies like other birds? What do owls do when there is snow on the ground? Can owls hear well?	(This section will be filled in as the unit progresses and facts are discovered.)

A Hoot of an Idea: Use three owls (enlarge page 29 three times) for creating the KWL Chart. Cut out the owls; label each owl; use them as directed above.

Know

Owls have big eyes.

Owls can fly.

Owls are birds.

Want to Know

When do owls look for food?

Do owls have nests?

Do owls have ears?

Learned

Most owls hunt for food at night.

Owls fly silently.

Owls can see well.

8

Story Mapping

See page 7, #1, for suggested use.

Sentence Strips

See page 7, #2 for suggested use.

Pa called to the Great Horned owl.	Late one winter night, Pa and I went out owling.	The owl flew quietly back into the woods.	We went deeper into the dark woods.	Pa said, "It is time to go home."

3 1833 04021 924 5

Sentence Strips *(cont.)*

See page 7, #2 for suggested use.

Pa and I silently walked toward the woods.

An echo could be heard coming through the trees when Pa called.

Our feet crunched on the crisp snow as we walked toward the woods.

A Great Horned owl was landing on a branch.

We stopped at a clearing deep in the dark woods.

Big Book

Big books are a great learning tool since they combine knowledge, language, reading, artwork, and presentation. Create a cooperative big book as a culminating experience for the retelling of *Owl Moon*.

Materials

- sentence strips (pages 10 and 11)
- glue
- scissors
- crayons, paints, or felt markers
- rulers, pencils, and erasers
- butcher paper or large sheets of drawing paper (12" x 18"/30 cm x 46 cm), 12 sheets total

Directions

1. Reproduce and cut out the sentence strips.
2. Have the children work cooperatively to put the strips in the story's sequential order.
3. Glue the strips near the bottom edge of the sheets (pages), one strip per page.
4. Have the children illustrate each page as the sentence strip indicates.
5. Stack the completed pages in sequential order. Add the remaining blank pages,—one for the front cover, the other for the back cover. Staple the pages together along the left-side edge to form the book's spine.

A Hoot of an Idea: Using the basic guidelines outlined above, have your children make up the text as well as the illustrations.

When You Go Owling...

When you go owling...

Time:_____

Place: _____

The woods will look_____.

The woods will feel _____.

The sounds you hear will be_____.

The owl will look _____.

Rules:

You have to be _____.

You will need _____.

You cannot _____.

Owly

by Mike Thaler

Summary

Owly acts like a typical two-year-old child, full of questions that are impossible to answer. Owly tries to find out how many stars are in the sky, how high the sky is, how many waves are in the ocean, and how deep the ocean is. Mother does not try to stop Owly from trying to find out the answers but rather encourages him to discover the answers for himself. Owly soon realizes that there are many things in his life that do not have exact answers—but one thing he is certain of is the love of his mother, as much as the sky is high and the ocean is deep.

The outline below is a suggested plan for using the various activities that are presented in this unit. You should adapt these ideas to fit your own classroom situation.

Sample Plan

Lesson 1

- Prepare a forest atmosphere (page 15, #1).
- Create a KWL chart, if you have not already done so (page 8).
- Begin to explore the concept of owls as an endangered species (page 77).
- Complete Save the Owls and design Save the Owls T-shirts (page 16, #3).
- Complete Preservation of Owls (page 16, #4).
- Read *Owly* and discuss the story.

Lesson 2

- Review *Owly*.
- Recite owl poems (page 23).
- Complete a thought web of owl facts (page 16, #6).
- Play Owly's Fact Game (page 22).
- Make paper plate owls (page 55).

Lesson 3

- Teach the Elements of a Story (page 26).
- Invent mixed-up owls and write stories about the new bird creations (page 17, #9).

- Complete the Owl Matching activity (page 35).
- Conduct the Graphing Owls exercise (page 50).
- Sing Owl Songs (page 56).

Lesson 4

- Explore the meanings of legends (page 27).
- Read An Owl Legend (page 28).
- Discover various owl habitats, using the Owl Reference Charts (pages 72–73) and complete the Owl Habitats sheet (page 51).
- Explore owl pellets by conducting Lesson 1 (page 37).
- Complete Owly's Word Search (page 32).

Lesson 5

- Conduct Owl Pellet Lessons 2 and 3 (pages 37–38).
- Play the Owl and Mice game (page 17, #12).
- Plan, prepare, and practice the owls thematic unit culminating activities (page 17, #13).
- Send A Hoot of a Time! invitations (page 78).

Overview of Activities

Setting the Stage

1. The atmosphere in your classroom will set the mood for this story and add to the thematic unit on owls. If you have not already done so, create an owls bulletin board and learning center area (page 70).

2. Show the cover of the book *Owly* and ask the children to predict what the events of the story might be. Their input into what they think the story will be about will help to build anticipation.

Enjoying the Book

1. When reading the story, periodically stop and discuss the events of the story so the children can fully appreciate the story content. (After reading the first two pages, show the children the pictures and discuss the main characters of the story.)

2. Lead a discussion about Owly's questions: How many stars are in the sky? How high is the sky? How many waves in the ocean? How deep is the ocean? Ask your children if Owly could find out the answers to these questions. Discuss what dangers a small owl might encounter on his journeys to answer these questions. Is it safe for a young bird/child to go out on his/her own? Should a grown-up owl like Owly's mother go with him? List their ideas and thoughts on chart paper.

3. Owly did think there was a definite answer to all his questions, but the only definite answer he got was that he loved his mother and his mother loved him "more than all the stars in the sky and as deep as the ocean." Maybe Owly has other questions. Encourage your children to brainstorm more questions Owly may want to have answered. With the children, decide if the answers could be easily discovered or would be too difficult for a young bird/child to answer by himself or herself.

4. Recite the owl poems and chant (page 23) for enjoyment as well as for vocabulary development.

5. Make certain the children become acquainted with facts about owls. The children will grow in knowledge by listening and viewing books and pictures of owls (see pages 79 and 80).

Extending the Book

1. Create a forest atmosphere around the door to your room. Have the children make branches and tree trunks on the sides of the doorframe, using brown bulletin board paper. Add a "canopy" of green leaves to the branches over the upper frame of the doorway. This special entry way will enhance the concept of saving the forest and protecting owls, which is discussed on pages 18 and 19.

Overview of Activities *(cont.)*

Extending the Book *(cont.)*

2. Create a chart entitled "Point of View." Encourage the children to recall the world from Owly's point of view and from his mother's point of view. List their responses on the chart.

Point of View		
Item	**Owly's Point of View**	**Mother's Point of View**
sky		
stars		
ocean		
love		

3. The concept of owls as an endangered species is outlined on page 77. The children can work individually or cooperatively to search out information on endangered owls and what is being done to protect them. Complete Save the Owls (page 18). The children choose five important ways to protect the owl population and list them on their papers. From the generated lists, they are to choose the one which they feel is the most important and design a "Save the Owls" T-shirt. Have the children create, color, and cut out their T-shirt designs using large, white construction paper. Display the T-shirts in your room, in the hallway, or in the library.

4. The Preservation of Owls activity (page 19) will cause the children to think about protecting owls. It is recommended that you teach, or review, how naturalists are presently trying to save owls (page 77).

5. Allot time on a daily basis for sharing journal entries (page 24) so that the children can share their original thoughts.

6. The Thought Web (page 25) will help your children organize their ideas for writing facts about owls on the owl writing sheet (pages 20 and 21). Once they have generated their facts, have them copy them onto their assembled owls.

7. Play Owly's Fact Game (page 22). It can be played in small or large groups. The children may need to refer to the displayed reference charts (pages 72 and 73) and KWL chart (page 8) if they cannot think of an answer.

Overview of Activities *(cont.)*

Extending the Book *(cont.)*

8. The graphic organizer, Elements of a Story (page 26), can be used for any story the children write. It may also be used for outlining a story about a mixed-up owl (page 26) or for creating a legend (page 27).

9. Have the children create a new kind of bird—a mixed-up owl (page 26). After they have created, drawn, and cut out their new bird creations, using white construction paper, add the birds to a bulletin board background scene. Be certain to label the birds with their mixed-up bird names.

10. Copy the owl reference charts (pages 72 and 73) for the children to use during the owl graphing exercise (page 50) where they will use crayons or markers to illustrate the heights of the owls, as well as their own heights, in a bar graph.

11. Read the An Owl Legend (page 28) to your children. Then have the children create their own legends (page 27).

12. Play the Owl and Mice game. Assign one child to be the owl. He or she sits in the middle of the "play area" as if perched in a tree or on a fence post. The remaining children are mice. They will place themselves in a safe spot referred to as "the nest," such as behind a line or on a small rug. The mice begin to creep out of their nest to search for food. When the "owl" hoots, "twit-ta-whoo, twit-ta-whoo," he or she tries to catch as many mice as possible (child playing the owl gently taps the children's shoulders) before they get back to their "nest." The mice that are caught become owls and help catch more mice until all of the mice are caught.

13. The culminating activities for this unit are designed to be a learning experience as well as an enjoyable time for both the presenters and the guests. Readers Theater (pages 65–69) does not need to be a polished activity; rather, the text is meant to be read from the script. An additional culminating activity can be presenting the flannelboard drama (pages 58–62). Enlarge the drama panels by using a photocopier or overhead projector; color, cut out and glue the panels to heavier flannel-backed paper. Invite an audience (invitations, page 78) and perform the Readers Theater and the Five Wise Owls flannelboard drama. Have some children act as naturalists and present oral reports about what has been learned during the owls thematic unit. Provide a tasty owl treat (recipes, page 63) as a snack before or after the performances.

Save the Owls

Write five ideas for saving owls. Put a star (★) next to the best idea.

1. _____

   _____

2. _____

   _____

3. _____

   _____

4. _____

   _____

5. _____

   _____

Draw a picture of the best idea in the box below.

Preservation of Owls

Read the sentences below. If the statement will help keep owls safe, draw a happy face ☺ in the box. If the statement will not help keep owls safe, draw a sad face ☹ in the box.

	Build homemade owl habitats.
	Stop pollution in the air and water.
	Catch owls for city zoos.
	Stop cutting down trees in forests.
	Build better roads and bigger cities.
	Set up injured owl treatment centers.
	Keep owls as pets.
	Inform people about how owls help people.
	Cut down trees so owls have more room.
	Stop the use of sprays that poison owls' food.
	Plant trees for the owls to live in.
	Let the owls take care of themselves.

A Hoot of an Idea: On the back of the paper, draw a picture of how you can help to save an owl's habitat.

Facts About Owls

20

Owl Wings

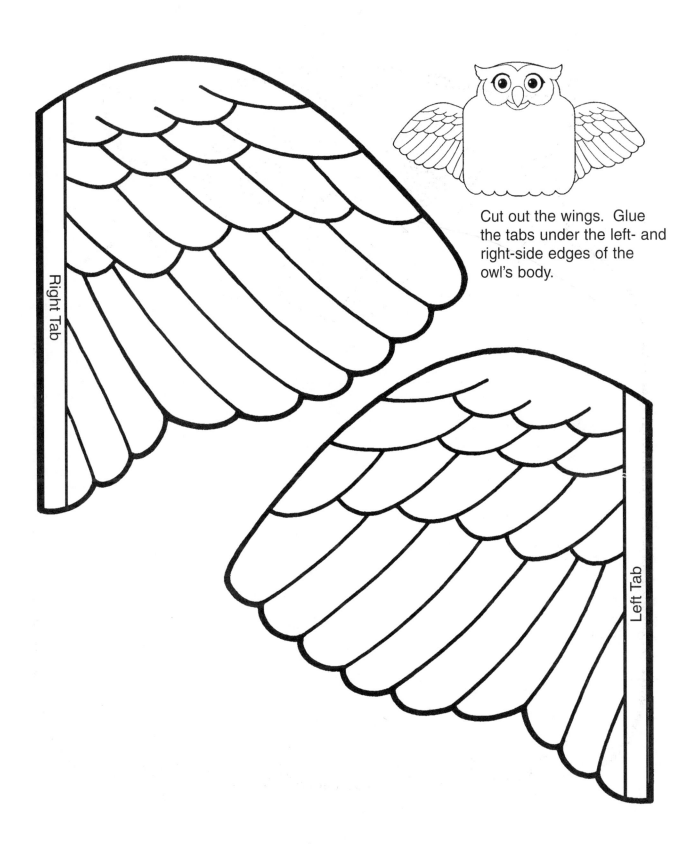

Cut out the wings. Glue the tabs under the left- and right-side edges of the owl's body.

Right Tab

Left Tab

Owly's Fact Game

Each fact square needs to be filled in by
having a different person fill in each square.
When all of your card's squares are filled in,
call out "Whoo-whoo!" If you are the first one
to hoot—you will be the winner!

An owl can s_____ and h_____ well.	Owls can be saved by... _____ _____ _____	An underground nest is a... _____	Most owls live... _____ _____ _____
Owls have w_____ and h_____ eyes.	The name of a very small owl is... _____	Owls talk by... _____ _____	The owl that lives in the Arctic is... _____
A Great Horned owl has t_____ on its head.	Endangered means... _____ _____	The _____ owl lives in a saguaro cactus.	Owls eat... _____ _____
Predators are... _____ _____ _____	The owl's talons are used for...	Owls sleep... _____ _____	Owl enemies are... _____ _____ _____

22

Owl Poems and Chant

Mr. Owl

A wide-eyed owl in an old oak tree,

Blinking and winking so quietly.

He sits and sleeps when the world is light,

Dreaming of what he'll catch tonight.

Then at dusk when the sun goes down,

He wakes and stretches and looks around.

A loud "tu-whit, tu-whoo" he cries,

He flaps his wings and away he flies.

A tasty mouse for an evening meal,

Or searches and prowls for another bite to steal.

When the first morning light is shed,

Away he'll fly to a comfortable bed.

The world of an owl, it's plain to see...

Is not the kind of life for me!

Owls Like Mice (*Chant*)

Owls like mice

Gray mice

Brown mice

Mean mice

Any kind of mice

Owls like mice!

A mouse in the grass

A mouse in a barn

A mouse in the trash

A mouse on the farm

I declare—anywhere

Owls like mice!

Owls like mice

Big mice

Small mice

Fat mice

Skinny mice

Sly mice

Silly mice

Owls like mice!

A Wise Old Owl (*An Action Poem*)

Oh, did you know that an owl is wise?

(*Encircle each eye with thumb and forefinger.*)

Winking and blinking its two big eyes.

(*Wink and blink your eyes.*)

With a beak that is a sharp-pointed nose,

(*Make your two forefingers point along the sides of your nose.*)

And talon claws for his sharp toes.

(*Make your fingers look like claws.*)

He sits up high on a branch in a tree,

(*Point upward with your forefinger.*)

And waits as quiet as quiet can be.

(*Put your forefinger in front of your lips.*)

He flaps his wings at both me and you,

(*Bend your elbows and flap your arms like wings.*)

And calls out a loud "whoo, whoo, wh-o-o!"

(*Make a megaphone with your hands cupped around your mouth.*)

Wise Owl

A wise old owl sat in an oak,

The more she saw, the less she spoke.

The less she spoke, the more she heard,

Why can't we all be like that wise old bird?

Writing Experiences

Personal Journal Writing

Encouraging children to keep a personal journal is a wonderful way to help them express written and oral language. Allow time daily for your children to write. If possible, also allow time for the children to share their writings by reading their entries to each other.

Keep in mind that these journals are personal. When you read a personal journal, it is to understand a child's thoughts. Do not focus on perfect penmanship or skill ability. When you read a child's personal journal, you should respond in writing on the given page(s) or orally communicate your comments if the child is an emergent reader. When you write or share your positive comments, a child is more excited about writing and takes pride in what he or she has written.

Journals can also serve as a child-centered authentic assessment that allows you to see whether taught skills have become strategies.

The owl pattern (page 29) can be used for individual writing activities or as a journal cover. For use as a cover, reproduce the pattern onto cardstock paper and cut out the owl. Stack lined or unlined paper for the interior pages of the journal; cut the pages in the same shape as the cover. Staple the cover to pages to form the owl journal.

Writing topics can vary greatly and may include some of the following ideas: interesting owl facts learned; personal feelings about, or experiences with, owls; summaries of activities completed during the owl unit; and imaginative stories about owls. The following story-starter ideas have been designed to encourage written expression:

1. Going Owling...Put yourself in the place of the child in the story *Owl Moon*. Write about your adventure.
2. If I had an owl for a pet, I would...
3. If I could be an owl for a day, I would...
4. My favorite owl is... Why?
5. If I took a baby owl home, my mom and dad would....
6. Select a famous fairy tale and rewrite the tale featuring an owl as the main character. Your story should begin with "Once upon a time..." and end with "They lived happily ever after."

Title Starters:

1. **The Owl Who Was Afraid of the Dark**
2. **Caring for Owls**
3. **The Owl That Could Not Hoot**
4. **The Owl That Could Not Sleep**
5. **I'm a Mixed-Up Owl (page 26)**
6. **Who-o-o Are You?**
7. **An Owling Adventure**

Writing Experiences *(cont.)*

Important Book Pattern

See page 7, #4 for suggested use.

Important Book Pattern

The important thing about _____

is that_____ .

It _____ .

It _____ .

It _____ .

It _____ .

It _____ .

It _____ .

But the most important thing about _____

is that it is _____ .

Thought Web

See page 16, #6 for suggested use.

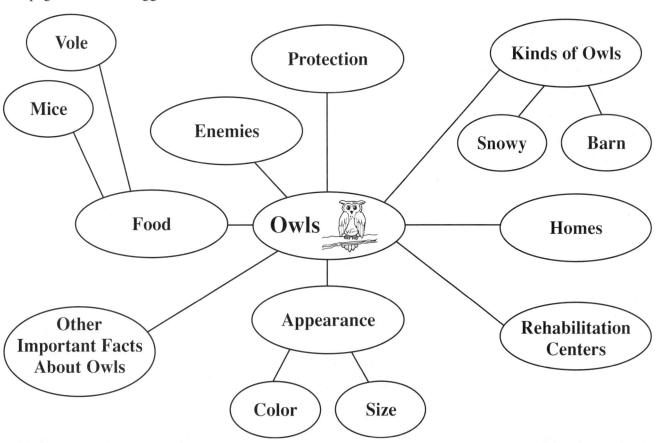

Writing Experiences *(cont.)*

A Mixed-Up Owl

See page 17, #9 for suggested use.

Owlican
(Owl + Pelican)

Owlurkey (Owl + Turkey)

Elements of a Story

Understanding the concept of the elements of a story helps children become better writers. They need to know that a story includes a title, an author, the setting, the characters, events, solving a problem, and a conclusion. The story line below is based on *The Wisest Answer* by David R. Collins (Milliken, 1987).

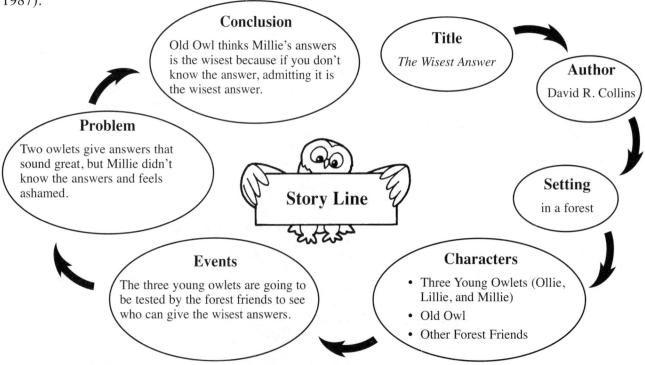

Conclusion
Old Owl thinks Millie's answers is the wisest because if you don't know the answer, admitting it is the wisest answer.

Title
The Wisest Answer

Author
David R. Collins

Problem
Two owlets give answers that sound great, but Millie didn't know the answers and feels ashamed.

Story Line

Setting
in a forest

Events
The three young owlets are going to be tested by the forest friends to see who can give the wisest answers.

Characters
• Three Young Owlets (Ollie, Lillie, and Millie)
• Old Owl
• Other Forest Friends

Writing Experiences *(cont.)*

Owl Chants

Enjoy the Owls like Mice chant (page 23). Then have the children make up their own chants about owls. Brainstorm owl-related words with the children, including words that describe owls, show the actions of owls, tell where owls live or find food, and tell what owls eat. Place the generated words on a chart and display them. Now have the children write their own chants.

Adjectives	Owl Actions	Places Owls Find Food	What Owls Like to Eat
graceful	fly	barn	mice
spotted	swoop	meadow	grasshoppers
fluffy	hoot	forest	rats
tiny	blink	stream	rabbits
plump	glide	field	skunks

Cinquain Poem

The prepared Owl Chants chart (above) may prove helpful in writing cinquain poetry.

Line 1—One noun
Line 2—Two describing words for owls
Line 3—Three words that give action to owls
Line 4—Four words that express feelings about owls
Line 5—One word that refers to the title (a different word)

Owls
Powerful, Awesome
Diving, Soaring, Swooping
Silently searching for food
Majestic

Legends

It is generally accepted that legends are the oral records of the world and its history. A legend is a popular type of folk story where animals and people speak the same language. Native-American people believe that spirits live in every part of nature. Page 28 is a Mohawk Indian legend. After reading the legend, have your children create "new" legends. Encourage them to use the elements of a story (page 26) as they are writing their legends.

Possible Legend Titles:

1. **Why the Owl Talks with a Hoot**

2. **How the Great Horned Owl Got Its Tufts**

3. **How the Owl Got Its Hooked Beak**

4. **How the Owl Got Big Eyes**

5. **Why the Owl Hunts at Night**

An Owl Legend

Why Rabbits and Owls Look the Way They Do

Adapted from How We Saw the World *by C. J. Taylor (Tundra Books, 1993)*

Long ago the Great Creator was making the forest animals. Each animal told him how it wanted to look and what it would do that would be special. The Great Creator listened carefully to each animal.

When it was Rabbit's turn, he said, "I want the longest ears and the best hop in all the world."

The Great Creator began to form Rabbit. He made his ears long and soft. He made his back legs long and strong. Then, just as he was starting to work on Rabbit's front legs, he was rudely interrupted by Owl. Owl was waiting in line.

"I want to tell you how I want to look," Owl said.

The Great Creator told Owl, "Please be patient and wait your turn."

But Owl kept right on talking. "I want the best of everything! I want the most colorful feathers, the longest neck, the smallest eyes, and a song that will make the other birds wish they could sing like me."

The Great Creator became annoyed. "I told you to wait your turn! It takes time to make every animal and bird special. Now stay in line. I will call you when I am ready."

"Who-o-o me?" asked Owl. "No-o-o. I'm staying right here."

"You will not!" shouted the Great Creator. He was so upset that he dropped Rabbit and grabbed Owl.

"Mr. Owl, you said you want colorful feathers? Yours will be gray and brown." He rubbed Owl's feathers with mud. "You want a long neck? You will not have a neck." He pushed Owl's head down into his body. "You want small eyes? You will have big eyes that only see well at night. You want to sing the prettiest songs? You will hoot the rest of your days."

Then the Great Creator turned back to work on Rabbit, but Rabbit had been so frightened when he was dropped by the Great Creator that he had run off to hide. Rabbit has never forgotten his fright and is still shy to this day.

Owl Pattern

Lunch with Owly

Unscramble the words, using the word bank below.

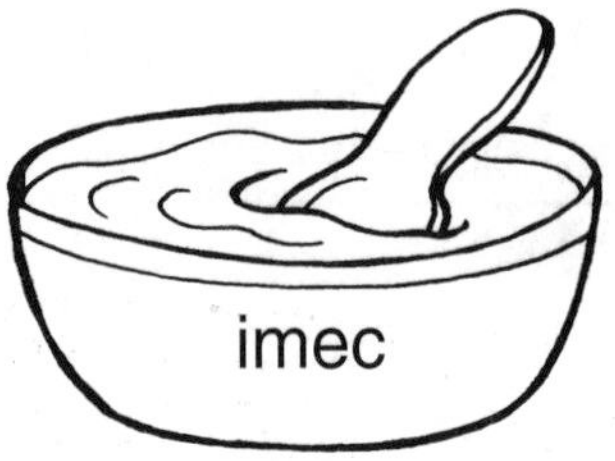

imec

hifs

1. _____

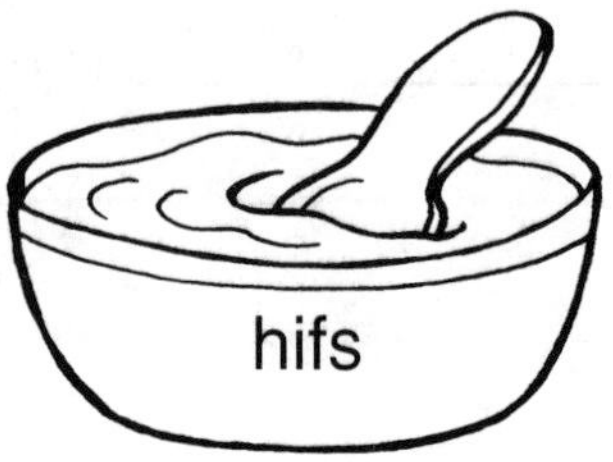

2. _____

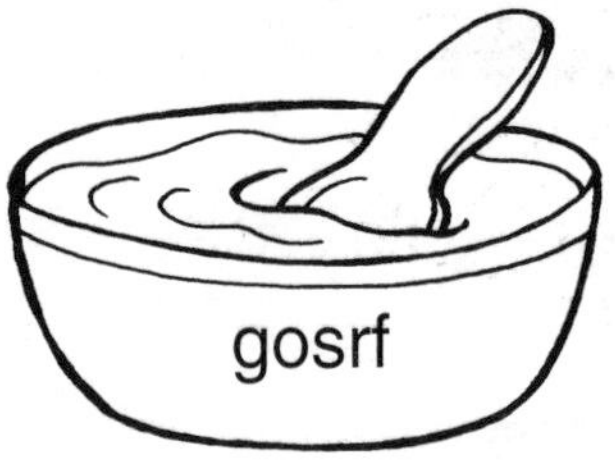

gosrf

moswr

mgslimen

3. _____

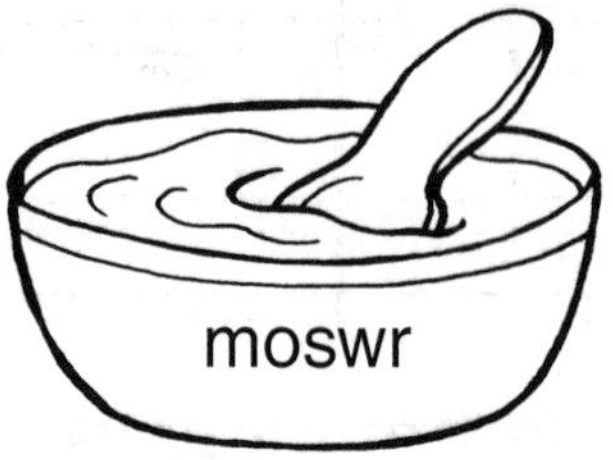

4. _____

5. _____

dribs

tsab

snetcis

6. _____

7. _____

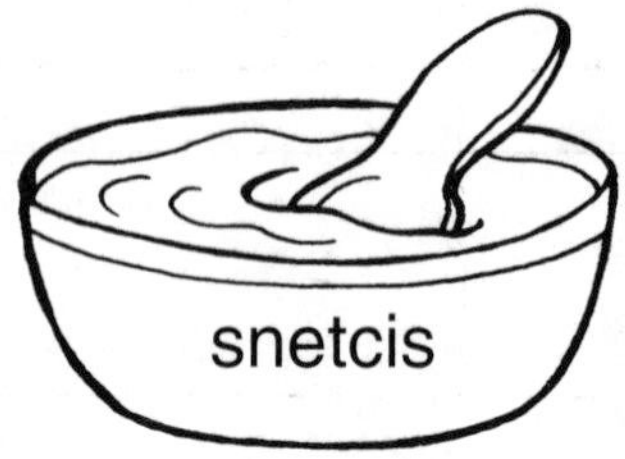

8. _____

srgaposhprse

ksanes

ruqrilses

9. _____

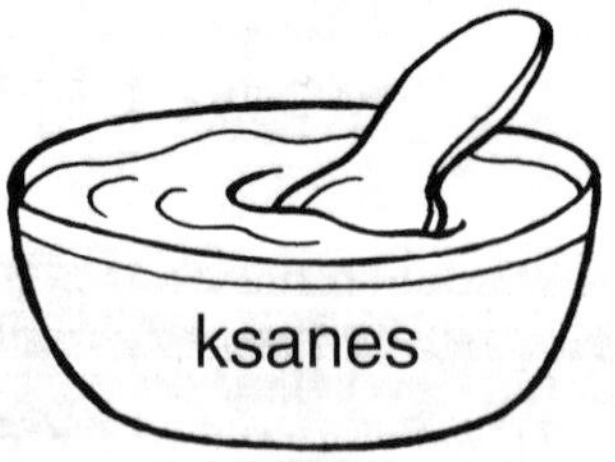

10. _____

11. _____

A Hoot of an Idea: On the back of this paper, draw a plate, a knife, and a fork. On the plate, draw some food you would like to eat for lunch.

Word Bank		
squirrels	bats	mice
worms	frogs	insects
birds	snakes	lemmings
grasshoppers	fish	

Owl Crossword Puzzle

Across

2. An owl _ _ n _ s for food at night.

5. Young owls have s _ _ t feathers.

6. An old hollow tree makes a good place for a n_ s _.

8. An owl has big _ y_ s.

9. An owl's _ _ _ k is hooked.

Down

1. A great lunch for an owl is a m _ _ s_.

3. Sharp t _ l _ _s tear the owl's prey.

4. An owl's warning call is a _ _ _ t.

7. Most owls s _ _ _ p during the day.

8. An owl's _ _ r _ are hidden under its head.

Owly's Word Search

Find the words related to owls in the puzzle below.

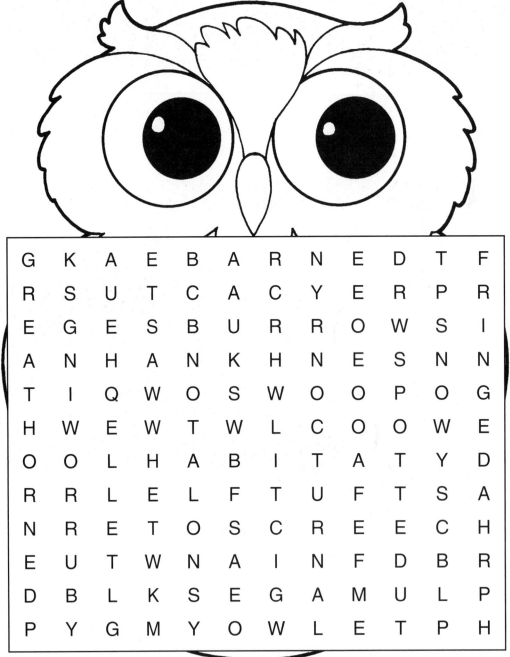

G	K	A	E	B	A	R	N	E	D	T	F
R	S	U	T	C	A	C	Y	E	R	P	R
E	G	E	S	B	U	R	R	O	W	S	I
A	N	H	A	N	K	H	N	E	S	N	N
T	I	Q	W	O	S	W	O	O	P	O	G
H	W	E	W	T	W	L	C	O	O	W	E
O	O	L	H	A	B	I	T	A	T	Y	D
R	R	L	E	L	F	T	U	F	T	S	A
N	R	E	T	O	S	C	R	E	E	C	H
E	U	T	W	N	A	I	N	F	D	B	R
D	B	L	K	S	E	G	A	M	U	L	P
P	Y	G	M	Y	O	W	L	E	T	P	H

BEAK	BURROWS	SPOTTED	NOCTURNAL
FRINGE	BURROWING	PYGMY	OWLET
PLUMAGE	SWOOP	SAWWHET	BARN
TUFTS	HOOT	ELF	CACTUS
WINGS	SCREECH	GREAT HORNED	HABITAT
TALONS	PREY	SNOWY	

32

Parts of an Owl

Use the words in the box to label the picture.

Word Box

beak	talons
wing	back
facial disk	tail
breast	chin
tuft	crown
eye	head

Comparing Bird Skeletons

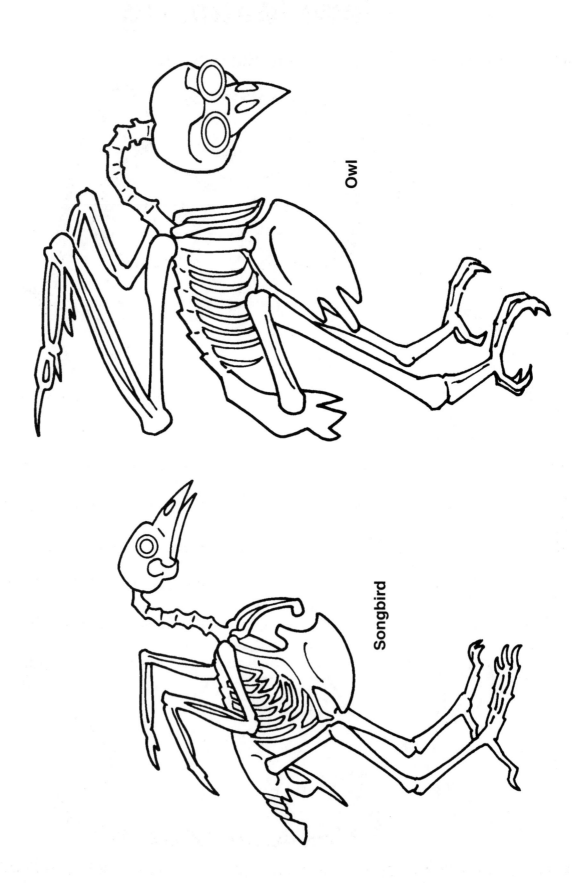

Owl

Songbird

Owl Matching

Match the owl names to the owls' descriptions.

1. Burrowing Owl

2. Snowy Owl

3. Barn Owl

4. Great Horned Owl

5. Screech Owl

6. Spotted Owl

7. Elf Owl

8. Great Grey Owl

_____feasts on lemmings

_____lives in old-growth forests

_____lives in a saguaro cactus

_____lives in burrows underground

_____has a heart-shaped head

_____makes a shrill whistle sound

_____largest owl in North America

_____has large feathery tufts on its head

A Hoot of an Idea: Use the owl charts (pages 72-73) to help you discover the correct matches.

Studying Owl Pellets

Teacher Information

Owls are birds of prey. They eat a diet of rodents, birds, and, occasionally, large insects such as grasshoppers. Owls eat their prey whole but cannot digest the bones, fur, or hard insect parts. They collect these indigestible parts in their stomachs, and the stomach muscles form these parts into a ball which the owls eventually spit out. The ball (pellet) resembles a cat's fur ball. Owl pellets usually contain the bones from several meals of animals, as well as fur and, sometimes, feathers.

Discoveries

- The study of an owl pellet reveals the particular diet of an owl.
- The pellet may reveal the bones of specific mammals or birds.
- The pellet may reveal the remains of two or more prey.

Owl Pellet Information

1. Since owl pellets contain fur, they often become infested with wool-eating moths. Older pellets may contain clothing-moth larvae and pupae. The larvae and pupae can be destroyed by enclosing the pellets in a jar with a few moth balls. Commercially prepared owl pellets have been fumigated to destroy any stages of clothing moths.
2. Owl pellets should be handled without gloves because it is easier to locate the tiny bones. Always make certain you wash your hands after handling the pellets.

Materials

- owl pellets (see page 80)
- large plastic container
- $1^3/_4$ pints (1 liter) water mixed with 2 tablespoons (30 mL) bleach
- plastic gloves

- tweezers
- paper towels
- Pellet Observation sheet (page 39)
- Bone Identification Key (page 40)
- Vole Skeleton Chart (page 41)

Owl Pellet Preparation

1. Place the owl pellets in the plastic container. Cover the pellets completely with the water-and-bleach solution. (It is suggested you wear plastic gloves for this process.) Soak the pellets for approximately one-half to one hour. Lift pellets out of the water with tweezers; allow them to dry on the paper towels.
2. Reproduce the Pellet Observation sheet, Bone Identification Key, and Vole Skeleton Chart, one per child.
3. Prepare the Bone Identification Key and Vole Skeleton Chart as an overhead transparency.
4. Each child or pair of children will need a small tray (a grocery store meat tray works well) containing the materials for all three lessons:

- tweezers
- softened owl pellet
- magnifying glass
- small plastic containers (empty film canisters work well)

- toothpicks
- dark-colored tagboard
- white glue
- paper towels
- plastic wrap

5. Review the three lessons (pages 37–38). You may choose to do one or all of them with your children.

Studying Owl Pellets *(cont.)*

Lesson 1: Observing an Owl Pellet

1. Show the children an owl pellet. Encourage them to observe it closely. Ask them if they know what it is. Explain what an owl pellet is and the part the owl pellet plays in the life of an owl (see Teacher Information, page 36).

2. Place the observed owl pellet onto an overhead projector and compare the size of an owl pellet to a paper clip (placed next to the owl pellet). Have the children make verbal observations about the size difference.

3. Prepare to dissect an owl pellet for demonstration, doing so directly on the overhead projector. Demonstrate how you must carefully pull apart the pellet using tweezers and toothpicks. Remind them that they will need to take great care when they do the same so that they will not break or destroy the bones in their pellets.

4. After the owl pellet has been dissected, have the children try to identify the bones and classify the bones (slip the Bone Identification Key transparency under the bones on the overhead projector). Have the children try to determine the size(s) of the animal(s) in the pellet.

5. Using the Vole Skeleton Chart overhead transparency, "pour" the bones from the Bone Identification Key transparency onto the Vole Skeleton Chart transparency. Do any of the bone sizes match? Discuss how owls eat a variety of animals which may explain the "extra" bones. Brainstorm other animals that the owl may have eaten.

6. As a closure to this lesson, discuss the benefits of having birds of prey such as owls. (Owls help to maintain the balance of nature by eating rodents that reproduce rapidly and destroy farmers' crops. Rodents can also carry disease, especially when they overpopulate an area.) A review of the Food Chain Chart (page 74) would help students retain these facts.

Lesson 2: Dissecting the Owl Pellet

1. The children can work individually or in pairs. Have the children cover their work area with paper towels. Review the use of the materials for the dissecting activity (see Lesson 1, Step #3, above).

2. Describe what the activity of dissecting owl pellets entails. Explain that an owl pellet is not feces, but they will need to wash their hands thoroughly when the lesson is finished. (If you prefer, provide plastic gloves for the children to wear during this lesson.)

3. Have the children gently pull apart the owl pellets using the tweezers and toothpicks. The children should very carefully feel for bones among the fur. When bones are found, encourage the children to remove the bones and place them in the provided plastic container. (**Note:** Toothpicks can be used to clean the fur from areas such as the skull(s) and vertebrae. The skull(s) may have to be put in water and washed a bit. Have the children study the bones closely by viewing them through magnifying glasses.)

Studying Owl Pellets *(cont.)*

Lesson 2: Dissecting the Owl Pellet *(cont.)*

4. Give a sheet of tagboard to each child or group of children. Have them pour their discovered bones onto the tagboard. Have them classify them by shape. After the children have classified their bones, have them circulate to view other groups' discoveries. Lead a large group discussion about what the owls ate. Record the ideas generated on a chart. (Do make certain the children realize that one owl pellet does not necessarily represent one meal. An owl can be forming an owl pellet in its stomach for a period of time during which it will have eaten three or four meals before regurgitating the pellet.) Have them complete the Pellet Observation sheet (page 39).

5. Have the children carefully store the contents of their pellets in the plastic containers for the next lesson.

Lesson 3: Reconstructing a Skeleton from the Owl Pellet Remains

Note: When the children begin to reconstruct the bones of the animal from the owl pellet they should be aware of the fact that not all of the bones of an animal will be present. The owl would have digested the softer bones. Only the hard bones, fur, uneaten portions of an animal, and, occasionally, feathers will be left in the pellet.

1. Distribute the Bone Identification Key (page 40) to the children, along with their owl pellet remains. Have the children begin to identify their bones as well as what type of animals were eaten by comparing the bones illustrated on the Bone Identification Key. (The task of sorting the bones may be difficult for some children so encourage them to use the tweezers and place the bones directly onto the Bone Identification Key illustrations.)

2. Have the children try to say the names of the bones. To motivate the children towards success, demonstrate using an overhead projector and the Bone Identification Key transparency so all can see the process. If you have them in your owl-pellet remains, locate a femur (leg bone) and a pelvis (hip bone), match them to the key and pronounce the names of these bones.

3. Have the children try to reconstruct an animal by using the reproduced tagboard Vole Skeleton Charts (page 41). Once they have matched as many of the bones as possible, have the children glue down the bones to the matching illustrations. (The glue will dry clear so the bones will be visible.) Have the children glue down any "extra" bones around the edges around the chart.

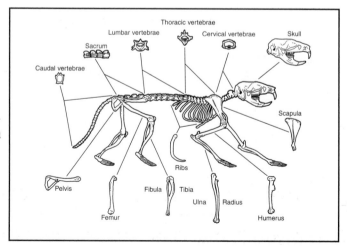

4. After the glue has hardened, have the children wrap their charts carefully with plastic wrap for preservation purposes. Display the charts for all to observe.

Pellet Observation

1. In the box below, sort the bones from your owl pellet by shape and then print in pencil what part of the body you think the bones came from.

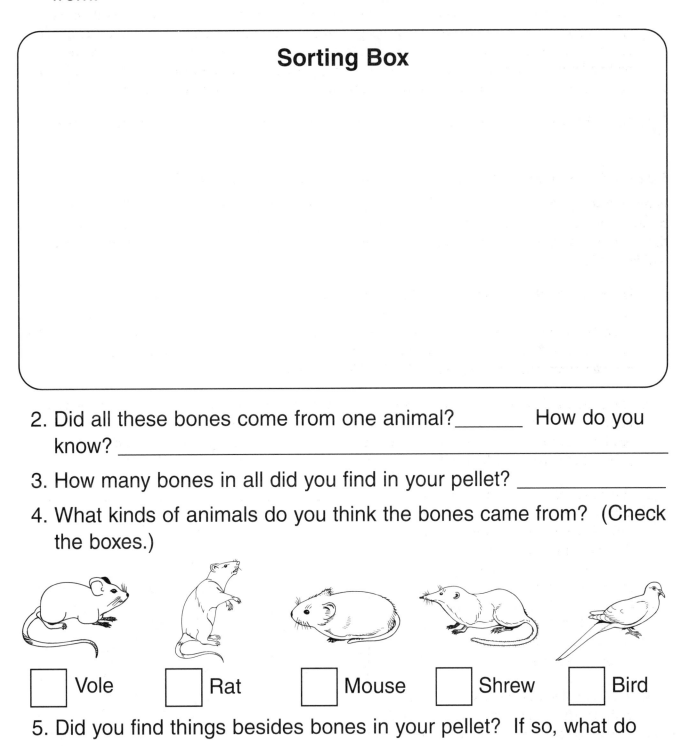

Sorting Box

2. Did all these bones come from one animal?_____ How do you know? _____

3. How many bones in all did you find in your pellet? _____

4. What kinds of animals do you think the bones came from? (Check the boxes.)

☐ Vole   ☐ Rat   ☐ Mouse   ☐ Shrew   ☐ Bird

5. Did you find things besides bones in your pellet? If so, what do you think they are? _____

Bone Identification Key

	Voles and Rats	Mice	Shrews	Birds
Skull and Jaws	Teeth	Tooth	Tooth	No Teeth
Hips (Pelvis)				
Shoulder (Scapula)	The shoulder blade is similar in all of these animals.			
Other	**Mole Skull and Jaw**	**Beetle Wings** **Insect Leg**	**Fish Bones** **Scales**	**Bird Breastbone** **Wing Bone**

Vole Skeleton Chart

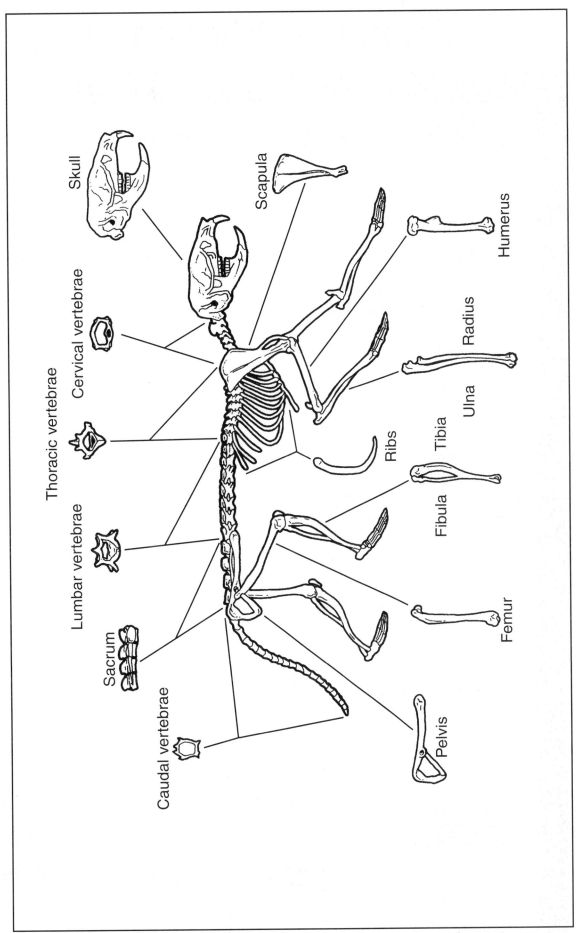

Studying Symmetrical Figures

Lesson 1: Studying Symmetrical Figures

Materials

- reproduced owl mask (page 46), one per child
- reproduced paper owl (pages 20 and 21, assembled)
- copies of the recording sheet (page 47), one per child
- pictures of various objects from magazines (some symmetrical, some asymmetrical)
- black large-tipped marker
- chart paper
- transparent tape

Directions

1. Show the prepared paper owl as well as the magazine pictures you have collected. Ask the children to generally describe what they see.
2. Show them the symmetrical paper owl again. Ask them what they notice about the left and right sides of the owl. Are they the same shape and size? Fold the owl in half vertically; unfold. Draw a long bold mark down the centerfold line with the black marker. Explain that one side of the owl picture is exactly like the other side. This is called *symmetrical*. Write the word *symmetry* on the left side of a sheet of chart paper. Share that when two sides are exactly the same, we say that the picture or object is symmetrical. Tape the owl to the left side of the chart paper.
3. Look again at the other pictures, one at a time, and ask the children to indicate if the two sides match when folded and re-opened. When they discover the first one that is not symmetrical, discuss that when two sides do not match, this is called *asymmetrical*. Add the word *asymmetry* to the right side of the chart paper. Tape the asymmetrical picture onto the right side of the chart paper. Go through all of the pictures and have the children classify the pictures by using the transparent tape to attach them in the correct column on the chart paper.
4. Have the children put on the prepared owl masks. (To make a mask, reproduce the pattern onto tagboard. Color and cut out the mask and eyeholes. Poke a hole through the small black dot on each side of the mask. Push a length of string through each hole; secure it.) Have the children look around the classroom or take a walk outside to discover and record both symmetrical and asymmetrical items on their recording sheets. When they see a symmetrical object, encourage them to call out "who-o-o, who-o-o" and point to that object. When your predetermined observing time is over, allow the children to compare lists.

Lesson 2: Making Symmetrical Figures

Materials

- scissors
- marker
- construction paper
- tempera paint (various colors)

Directions

1. Show the children how to make symmetrical figures. Fold a piece of paper in half. Draw half of a symmetrical heart with the marker (as shown). Cut along the object's outline, unfold, and display.
2. Have the children look again at their owl masks (see Lesson 1, above). Ask the children to fold their masks in half vertically along the beak and reopen to notice the masks' symmetry.

Studying Symmetrical Figures *(cont.)*

Lesson 2: Making Symmetrical Figures *(cont.)*

3. Provide the children with the materials needed (construction paper and tempera paints) to make their own symmetrical figures.

4. Ask them to fold their provided construction paper in half, press hard along the fold line, and then open it.

5. Demonstrate how they will make a symmetrical paint design. Dab small amounts of paint on or near the fold line. Close the paper along the fold line and press gently over the entire surface area. Unfold the paper to discover a symmetrical design. Now have the children create their own symmetrical designs. Allow the paint to dry thoroughly; display the creations.

6. For a writing extension, have the children decide what their shapes look like and write a story about the person, place, or thing that their shapes most resemble.

Lesson 3: Illustrating Symmetry with Pictures

Materials

*   catalogs and magazines
*   scissors
*   sheets of paper
*   glue
*   pencils, erasers, and crayons

Directions

1. Divide the children into small groups; provide each group with a supply of magazines and catalogs.

2. Have each child locate and cut out a picture that illustrates symmetry. Have each child fold his or her picture in half, open it, and cut the picture down the center line. Discard the right half of the cut picture.

3. Provide each child with a sheet of paper. Instruct the children to glue the saved left-half side of the cut picture onto the left side of the paper.

4. The children now draw the missing halves of their pictures, noting the details of the glued half.

A Hoot of an Idea: Have the children locate additional symmetrical pictures from magazines and cut them out. Cut all of the pictures in half and mix up all all of the halves. Allow the children to play a game of putting the pictures back together by matching the halves. (This idea makes a great learning center activity.)

Studying Symmetrical Figures *(cont.)*

Lesson 4: Creating Symmetrical Shapes

Materials

- reproduced geometrical shapes sheet (page 45), one or more per child
- a sheet of paper with a vertical line drawn down the center, one sheet per child
- scissors
- glue

Directions

1. Provide each child with a prepared sheet of paper and a geometrical shapes sheet.

2. Have each child cut out his or her own desired geometrical shapes to be placed just to the left of the center line; glue down these shapes.

3. Each child then cuts out matching shape, places them on the right side of the center line to complete the symmetrical picture and glue them into place.

A Hoot of an Idea: Make detailed symmetrical pictures using a variety of the cutout geometrical shapes. Here are a few examples:

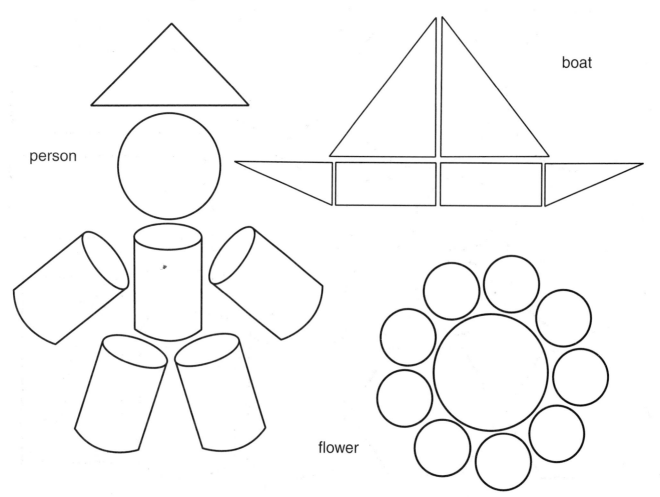

person

boat

flower

Geometrical Shapes

Owl Mask

See page 42, Step #4 for suggested use.

Cut Out

Cut Out

Who-o-o or What Did You See?

Draw a picture of what you have seen in the chart below.

Symmetrical Things	Asymmetrical Things

Owl Families of Number Facts

The term "number families" means number facts that are related because they have the same sum. An example of a number 3 family is

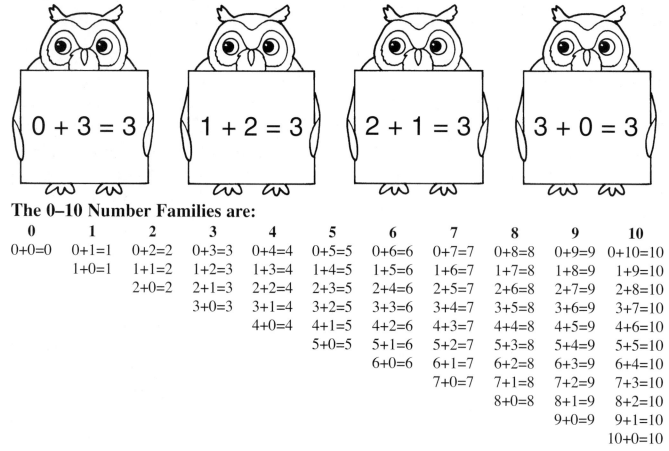

$0 + 3 = 3$ $1 + 2 = 3$ $2 + 1 = 3$ $3 + 0 = 3$

The 0–10 Number Families are:

0	1	2	3	4	5	6	7	8	9	10
0+0=0	0+1=1	0+2=2	0+3=3	0+4=4	0+5=5	0+6=6	0+7=7	0+8=8	0+9=9	0+10=10
	1+0=1	1+1=2	1+2=3	1+3=4	1+4=5	1+5=6	1+6=7	1+7=8	1+8=9	1+9=10
		2+0=2	2+1=3	2+2=4	2+3=5	2+4=6	2+5=7	2+6=8	2+7=9	2+8=10
			3+0=3	3+1=4	3+2=5	3+3=6	3+4=7	3+5=8	3+6=9	3+7=10
				4+0=4	4+1=5	4+2=6	4+3=7	4+4=8	4+5=9	4+6=10
					5+0=5	5+1=6	5+2=7	5+3=8	5+4=9	5+5=10
						6+0=6	6+1=7	6+2=8	6+3=9	6+4=10
							7+0=7	7+1=8	7+2=9	7+3=10
								8+0=8	8+1=9	8+2=10
									9+0=9	9+1=10
										10+0=10

Hootie-Hoot-Hootie Game

Preparation

Create owl number family facts cards by reproducing the facts from the 3 through 10 number families above onto small index cards.

Directions (*This game is similar to the card game Rummy.*)

1. Randomly shuffle the owl fact cards. Deal facedown five cards to each player. (Players may look at their cards.)

2. Place the remaining cards facedown in a pile on a flat surface; turn one card faceup beside the deck of cards.

3. The first player draws a card from the top of the deck. The player may keep that card and discard one that he or she is already holding, trade it with the faceup card next to the deck of cards, or simply discard the one just picked up. The players continue to take turns as explained in this step.

   When it is a specific player's turn and he or she is holding an owl family of four related family facts, he or she puts down the owl family set and calls out, "Hootie-hoot-hootie!" The player then draws four new cards from the top of the deck.

4. When no more fact families of four can be made, the players count up their laid-down card sets. The one with the most displayed sets wins.

48

Spotty Owl's Problem Solving

Draw pictures to help answer Spotty Owl's problems.

For example: Spotty Owl ate 3 mice, 2 insects, and 2 grasshoppers. How many did he eat in all?

 + = 7   3 + 2 + 2 = 7

---

1. Owls eat insects. Spotty Owl ate 4 grasshoppers, 2 moths, and 3 pine beetles. How many insects did Spotty eat?

_____ + _____ + _____ = ☐

2. Spotty's habitat is disappearing. If men cleared 5 trees in the morning and 4 trees in the afternoon, how many trees did they clear in a day?

_____ + _____ = ☐

3. Spotty saw 3 hikers with packs and 4 with cameras. How many hikers did he see?

_____ + _____ = ☐

4. Spotty caught 4 mice. Screechy caught 3 mice. How many more mice did Spotty catch than Screechy?

_____ − _____ = ☐

5. Everyone must be careful not to hurt an owl's habitat. If 4 owls live in the forest and 3 are forced to leave, how many will be left?

_____ − _____ = ☐

6. If Spotty Owl eats 3 animals a day, how many will he eat in 3 days?

_____ + _____ + _____ = ☐

A Hoot of an Idea: Make up a story problem of your own on the back of this paper. If you have time, find a friend to read and work your problem.

Graphing Owls

Measure how tall you are. Color in the boxes in the first column until you reach your height. Then color in the owls' heights in the remaining columns.

60 in. / 120 cm							
55 in. / 110 cm							
50 in. / 100 cm							
45 in. / 90 cm							
40 in. / 80 cm							
35 in. / 70 cm							
30 in. / 60 cm							
25 in. / 50 cm							
20 in. / 40 cm							
15 in. / 30 cm							
10 in. / 20 cm							
5 in. / 10 cm							
	Myself	Elf Owl	Snowy Owl	Barn Owl	Great Horned Owl	Spotted Owl	Burrowing Owl

Which owl is the tallest? _____ Which owl is the shortest? _____

Are you taller than the tallest owl? _____ How much taller are you? _____

#2375 Thematic Unit—Owls   50   © Teacher Created Materials, Inc.

Owl Habitats

Draw four different owl habitats (homes) in the big wheel. Write the names of the owls that live in the four habitats in the small ovals.

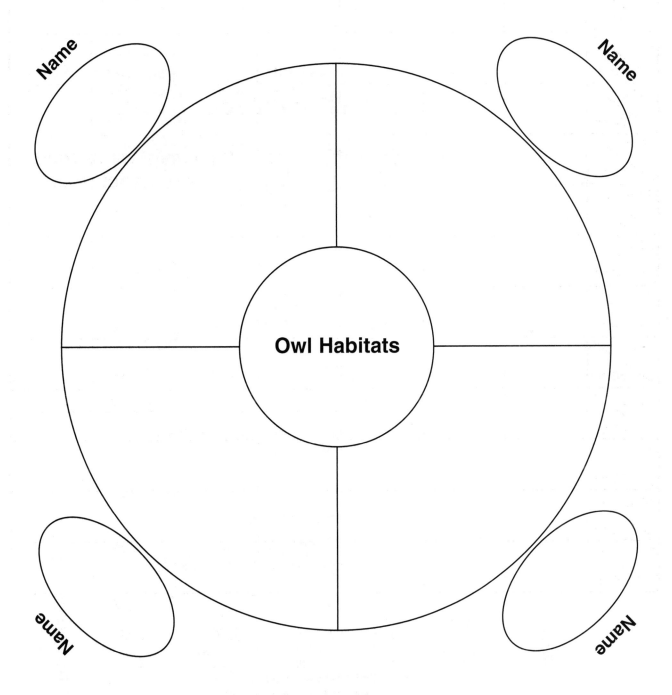

A Hoot of an Idea: On the back of your paper, draw a brand new type of habitat for an owl.

Owl Art Activities

Pine Cone Hooty Owl

Preparation

If possible, take the class for a walk or a field trip in the woods to gather pine cones for this art project. If this is not possible, use purchased pine cones.

Materials (per child)

- one small pine cone
- one large pine cone
- small tree branch or piece of driftwood
- felt scraps
- two small craft eyes
- glue
- scissors
- thread or fishing line

Directions

1. Glue the small pine cone horizontally to the broad end of the large pine cone. Allow the glue to dry thoroughly. (**Note:** You may have to trim the smaller pine cone so that it will sit properly on top of the large pine cone.)

2. Glue the craft eyes in place on the bottom (flat end) of the top pine cone.

3. Using the scissors and felt scraps, cut out a beak, talons (claws), ear tufts, and wings; glue them onto the two pine cones appropriately.

4. Glue the small tree branch or driftwood to the bottom of the larger pine cone; allow it to dry thoroughly.

5. Attach the thread or fishing line to the top of the owl's head by "catching it" onto one of the pine cone's scales so it can be hung as a decoration or ornament.

Thumbprint Owls

Materials

- black-ink stamp pad
- sheets of paper
- thin, black felt-tipped pen
- paper towels

Directions

1. Push your fingertip gently onto the ink pad.

2. Place the inked finger onto a sheet of paper; press until desired print is achieved. (Use the paper towels to wipe fingers off if they get too messy.)

3. Using the thin, black felt-tipped pen, add features and details to create the owls' body features and habitats.

Owl Art Activities *(cont.)*

Owl Place Mat

Materials

- light-brown construction paper (9" x 12"/23 cm x 30 cm)
- dark-brown construction paper strips (¹/₂" x 6"/1.3 cm x 15 cm)
- yellow, orange, and black construction-paper scraps
- blue construction paper (9" x 12"/23 cm x 30 cm)
- scissors
- glue

Preparation

Prepare the owl weaving patterns by first reproducing the owl weaving pattern (page 54) onto the light-brown contruction paper and cut out the outline owl shape. Then, using the scissors cut along the dashed lines.

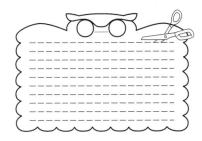

Directions

1. Using the dark-brown strips and an under-and-over weaving pattern, thread the strips across the "stomach" of the owl. (If your first strip goes *over-under*, the second strip will need to go *under-over*.)

2. Glue the ends of the strips to the back of the owl.

3. Cut two 1" (2.54 cm) diameter circles from the yellow scrap paper; glue them to the owl's eye sockets. Cut two ³/₄" (2 cm) diameter circles from the black paper; glue them down, centered, on top of the two yellow circles.

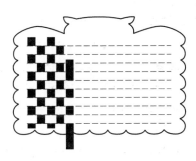

4. For the beak, cut a small diamond shape out of orange construction paper. Fold the diamond shape in half horizontally so that it looks like a triangular beak. Glue the beak on the owl's face by placing glue on the fold line and attaching the beak to the black line in between the owl's eyes.

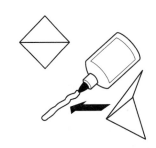

5. Glue the woven owl to a sheet of blue construction paper; allow it to dry.

6. Laminate the finished place mat for durability, if desired. (**Note:** If you choose to do this, the beak will no longer be three-dimensional.)

A Hoot of an Idea: Use the place mats during your culminating activities (page 64).

Owl Art Activities *(cont.)*

Owl Weaving Pattern

Owl Art Activities *(cont.)*

Owl Silhouette

Materials
- tagboard paper
- newspaper
- white construction paper
- toothbrush
- small container of water
- black watercolor paint
- craft stick

Directions
1. Create an owl pattern on tagboard paper; cut out the pattern.
2. Cover the work area with newspaper. Place the white construction paper on the newspaper.
3. Place the cutout owl pattern on the white construction paper.
4. Dip the toothbrush into the container of water and then into the black watercolor paint. (**Caution:** The toothbrush needs only a little bit of paint on it, or it will splatter big drops and not be as effective.)
5. Hold the toothbrush bristles downward over the construction paper. Using the craft stick, brush the stick across the bristles, moving the stick towards you; repeat. Continue this process with a few more dips into the water and black paint. When you have achieved the desired effect, allow the painting to dry. Remove the owl pattern.

Paper Plate Owl

Materials
- 8" or 9" (20 cm or 23 cm) ribbed-edge paper plate
- paintbrush
- brown watercolor paint
- yellow, black, light-brown, and orange construction-paper scraps
- cotton ball

Directions
1. Paint the paper plate with the brown watercolor paint. (**Note:** If the paint does not adhere to the paper plate, add a little bit of dishwashing detergent to the paint.) Allow the paper plate to dry.
2. Cut the owl's forehead from the light-brown paper. Create a square approximately 9" x 9" (23 cm x 22 cm). Fold the square from corner to corner to make two folded triangles. Glue the tip of one triangle to the front of the plate and the other triangle tip to the back of the owl's head (the construction paper fold will "rest" on the paper plate's edge).
3. Make tail feathers from light-brown construction paper and talons from orange construction paper with scissors cutting freehand; glue them into place.
4. Make the beak from orange construction paper and glue it onto the owl's face. Use the cotton ball to create a fluffy throat; glue it under the beak.
5. Make two $1\frac{1}{2}$" (3.84 cm) black circles for the outer eyes and two $\frac{3}{4}$" (2 cm) yellow circles for the inner eyes and glue them into place.

Owl Songs

Mr. Owl

(Sung to the tune of *Twinkle, Twinkle, Little Star*)

Hooting loudly from the trees,
Scolding creatures that he sees.
He's unfriendly, wears a frown,
Sends a message to all around.
Hooting, hooting down at me,
All alone he hoots with glee.
Keep your distance, don't come near,
He's not a toy, but do not fear.
He sleeps by day and hunts at night,
All small creatures run in fright.
He sits and blinks his two big eyes,
The owl is shy, but very wise.

A Wise Old Owl

(Sung to the tune of *Buffalo Gals*)

A wise old owl sat in a tree,
In a tree, in a tree.
Wide awake and winking was he.
Not making any sound.

Chorus
He spied two bunnies running past,
Hurry past, scurry past.
Heard a woodchuck rustle past,
And one wee country mouse.

But when a wind came whirling through,
Swirling through, twirling through,
"Ta-whooo," said he, "ta-whit, ta-whooo!"
Hoot, hoot, hoot.

Chorus
The wise old owl flew far away,
Far away, far away.
In search of food, no time to play,
By the light of the silvery moon.

Owls Are Sleeping

(Sung to the tune of *Frére Jacques*)

Owls sleeping, owls sleeping,
In a tree, in a tree,
No one's a-blinking, not even winking,
Down at me, down at me.

Owls

(Sung to the tune of *I'm a Little Teapot*)

I am a little barn owl,
Dressed in white.
Here is my heart face,
And eyes so bright.
When I go out hunting
In the night,
I hoot, hoot, hoot,
Til morning light.
I'm a tiny Elf owl,
Very small.
My home you'll find
In a cactus tall.
I am a hunter,
Day and night.
My feathers fringed
For quiet flight.
I'm a Great Gray owl,
Very grand.
I'm the largest owl
Across the land.
I sit a-staring,
From a forest tree.
I'm looking for a feast,
Wild and free.
I'm a Great Horned owl
With tufts on top.
I roam all over,
I never stop.
I feast on rodents,
Big and small.
I who-who-hoot,
That is my call.

Owl Drama

Whooo? Choral Poem

(**Note:** Encourage the children to use varying tonal qualities to add dramatics to the choral poem reading.)

Owl:　　Who-o-o hoots high in a forest tree,
　　　　　Watching the forest so carefully?

Children:　An owl stares with two big eyes,
　　　　　　Sits and blinks and looks so wise.

Owl:　　Who-o-o sleeps by day and hunts by night,
　　　　　When all small creatures run in flight?

Children:　An owl sits dozing all the day,
　　　　　　He dreams of feasts that are far away.

Owl:　　Who-o-o nests in a hole, a barn, or a tree,
　　　　　Quietly perched so peacefully?

Children:　An owl sleeps, eyes unblinking,
　　　　　　Maybe he's sleeping or maybe he's thinking.

Owl:　　Who-o-o has a strong beak and great broad wings,
　　　　　To swoop and grab many tiny things?

Children:　An owl with wings so widely spread,
　　　　　　Searching and hunting way overhead.

Owl:　　Who-o-o has eyes so big and round,
　　　　　Huge and staring, scanning the ground?

Children:　An owl peering into the yellow moonlight,
　　　　　　Watching for stirring in the deep dark night.

Owl:　　Who-o-o has talons as sharp as saws,
　　　　　Tearing, ripping, mighty claws?

Children:　An owl has such fearful hooks,
　　　　　　For catching food in deep forest nooks.

Owl:　　Who-o-o has marvelous, fringed-like feathers,
　　　　　For quietly flying in all kinds of weathers?

Children:　An owl has feathers for quiet flight,
　　　　　　They help surprise its prey at night.

Owl:　　Who-o-o is the night worker by the light of the moon,
　　　　　And sleeps in the day—way past noon?

Children:　An owl in his finely feathered dress,
　　　　　　Stately rules the forest crest.

Five Wise Owls

5 wise owls
Perched on a door.
1 flapped his wings
And then there were 4.

4 wise owls
Sat down to tea.
1 spilt his tea.
Oops! Then there were 3.

3 wise owls
Hooted who, who, whoooo!
1 lost his voice
And then there were 2.

2 wise owls
Could not find any fun.
"I am going to nap."
And then there was 1.

1 lonely owl
Saw the rising sun.
Flew off to his home
and then there was none!

Flannelboard Drama

5 wise owls perched on a door.

1 flapped his wings and then there were 4.

Flannelboard Drama *(cont.)*

4 wise owls sat down to tea.

1 spilt his tea.

Oops! Then there were 3.

Flannelboard Drama *(cont.)*

3 wise owls hooted who, who, whoooo!

1 lost his voice and then there were 2.

60

Flannelboard Drama *(cont.)*

2 wise owls could not find any fun.

"I am going to nap." And then there was 1.

Flannelboard Drama *(cont.)*

1 lonely owl saw the rising sun.

Flew off to his home and then there was none!

Owly Recipes

Owl Nests

Ingredients

- ¹/₂ cup (4 oz./225 g) peanut butter
- 12 oz. (350 g) chocolate chips
- 12 oz. (350 g) butterscotch chips
- 12 oz. (350 g) chow mein noodles
- 16 oz. (450 g) jelly bean candies

Directions

Melt the peanut butter, chocolate chips, and butterscotch chips in a pan over low heat, stirring constantly. Once melted, add the noodles and mix well to coat. Drop the coated noodles by spoonfuls onto waxed paper. Shape the noodles into "bird nests," using your thumb to make a slight indentation in the center. Place a few jelly beans in the center to represent eggs. Place the owls' nests in the refrigerator to harden.

Owl-Shaped Snack

Ingredients

- lettuce leaf, washed and dried
- 1 canned pear half (body)
- sliced bananas (eyes)
- Mandarin orange wedges (tufts)
- 1 raisin (beak)
- 1 black licorice strip (branch)

Directions

Place the lettuce leaf on a plate; add the pear half, centered, on top the lettuce leaf. Decorate the owl as illustrated.

Mouse Salad for an Owl

- 1 large lettuce leaf, washed and dried
- 1 canned pear half
- 2 slices of banana
- 1 slice cheese, slivered
- ¹/₂ of a maraschino cherry
- 2 raisins

Directions

Arrange ingredients on the leaf, using the pear half for the mouse's body, banana slices for ears, raisins for eyes, cherry for a nose, and cheese slivers for whiskers and tail, as illustrated.

A Hoot of a Time!

In the story *Owl Moon,* the young child and his pa went out owling in the forest (see page 5). For a culminating activity, plan an owling in your room where parents, administrators, and other children can come to learn about owls and join in on some owling activities.

Create an Owling Atmosphere

1. Reproduce and distribute invitations (page 78) to let your guests know when, where, and who-o-o is presenting the owling.

2. Display your KWL chart (page 8) or other informational charts (pages 72–75) and completed child-created art projects (pages 52–55) as decorations around the room; also freshen up your bulletin board display and learning center area (page 70).

3. If you have not already done so, prepare the props for the Readers Theater (pages 65 and 66), and begin practicing the "Owl at Home" script (pages 67–69).

4. Prepare "owl" foods (page 63) and make owl place mats (pages 53 and 54) that your guests can enjoy eating their snacks on. Be certain you have enough plates, utensils, napkins, drinks, and cups for all your guests.

5. Make the owl masks (page 46) for your children to wear while greeting the guests when they arrive for the owling.

6. Have your children record the owl chant (page 23) onto a cassette tape and have the tape playing as your guests arrive.

Consider these Owling Activities

1. Have a group of children show what was learned during your owl pellet lessons and what they discovered in the pellets. Have them show their completed Vole Skeleton Charts (Lesson 3, page 38). An actual demonstration of dissecting an owl pellet can be presented by a child using the overhead projector (as was demonstrated in Lesson 1, page 37).

2. Prepare to present the flannelboard drama (pages 58–62) by practicing the poem and reproducing the flannelboard panels (page 17, #13). Some children can recite the poem while others display the appropriate flannelboard panels.

3. Present the Readers Theater "Owl at Home" (pages 65–69).

4. Present the owl poems (page 23), or have everyone sing along to the owl songs (page 56) by displaying the words on large chart paper.

5. Play the Owl and Mice game (page 17, #12).

6. Present a gift that has been made by your children (art suggestions, pages 52–55) to each guest as a way of saying thank you for coming.

Readers Theater

Readers Theater is an excellent way to provide your children with the opportunity to perform a play with minimal rehearsal time, props, costumes, and sets. The children read the dialogue for the characters from the prepared script; therefore, memorization is not necessary.

Preparation

1. There are five parts in the play *Owl at Home*: Mr. Owl, Snow, Wind, Narrator, and Sound Maker. The Narrator and the Sound Maker do not use puppet props. The narrator reads the script from behind the stage (see #2 below) while the Sound Maker makes appropriate sounds (also from behind the stage area). The Sound Maker sounds are indicated by *italics* in the script. Assign the five parts yourself or hold an audition.

2. Create a puppet theater stage like the one shown below. You can use a cardboard carton that has been cut open (cut off one side section) and made into a three-sided structure, or you can purchase a science fair display board (available at most educational resource stores). In the center of the middle panel, cut a window opening, large enough to permit the puppets to be easily seen by the audience. Decorate the outside of the cardboard theater to show a winter scene.

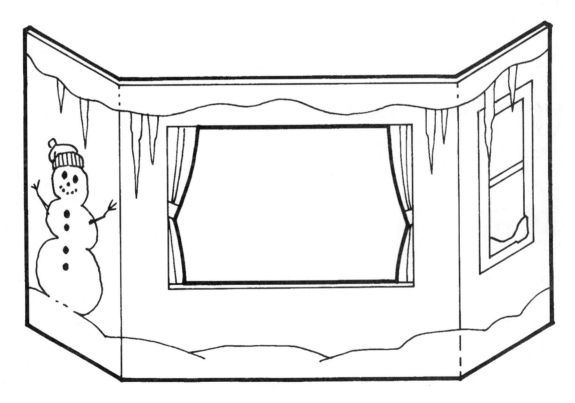

3. Reproduce and enlarge the puppets for the play (page 66). The enlargement process can be done with an opaque projector or a photocopier. Color the reproduced puppets, cut them out, glue them to heavier paper or cardboard and trim them. Attach the puppets to craft sticks so they can be easily held.

Readers Theater Props

Mr. Owl

Snow

Wind

Owl at Home Script

Narrator: Once upon a time there was an old owl who-o-o-o lived by himself in a small house deep in the woods. He was very happy. He enjoyed his life, safe from the cold winter storms. Let's visit Mr. Owl. . .I think I see him sitting in his easy chair.

Mr. Owl: I love to sit by my hot fire. It's so cold outside. I also love eating my buttered toast and hot pea soup.

(Knock, knock!)

Mr. Owl: Now who-o-o could that be on such a cold and snowy night?

(Knock, knock!)

Mr. Owl: I'd better answer the door. I'm sure who-o-o-ever it is must be frozen stiff.

(A louder knock, knock!)

Mr. Owl: (*An opening-the-door sound.*) Who-o-o is out there banging on my door? Hmm, no one is here. I'm sure I heard someone knocking.

Wind: Sw-i-s-h! We are here! Sw-i-s-h!

Mr. Owl: Who-o-o are you? I can't see you.

Snow: Br-r-r-r, we are freezing cold! Icicles are forming on our noses. We want to sit by a warm fire.

Mr. Owl: (*A closing-door sound.*) That's funny. I'm sure I heard someone, but I didn't see anyone. I only saw snow and wind.

Narrator: Mr. Owl slowly walks back to his easy chair by the fire. He picks up his soup and favorite book when...

(A loud bang-bang sound.)

Mr. Owl: Now who-o-o can that be banging on my door?

Narrator: (*A squeaking door-hinge sound.*) Mr. Owl opens the door just enough to peek out. Mr. Owl is beginning to get worried.

Mr. Owl: Who-o-o is there?

Wind: We-e-e are here! We are very c-c-c-cold!

Snow: It's fre-e-e-ezing out here! C-c-c-can we come in?

Mr. Owl: Hmmm, no one is here but poor old winter!

(A closing-door sound.)

Narrator: Mr. Owl hears more loud banging at the door. He is becoming getting annoyed. He has been interrupted so many times now that his soup is cold!

(A loud knocking sound.)

Owl at Home Script *(cont.)*

Mr. Owl: Who-o-o can that be? An owl can't even finish his supper. (*An opening-the-door sound.*) Wind and Snow, are you knocking at my door? Why don't you come in and sit down by my fire?

**Wind and
Snow:** We would like to come in and sit for awhile.

Mr. Owl: Come in then. You are welcome in my house.

Snow: It will be great to warm our toes by your fire.

Wind: Yes, wonderful! Thank you, Mr. Owl.

Narrator: Mr. Owl opens the door wide enough to let his two frozen guests in. (*A sqeaky-door-hinge sound.*) They come in his house with a frozen blast of air that almost pushes Mr. Owl off his feet.

Mr. Owl: Slow down, slow down! I know you're cold, but don't wreck my house!

Snow: Mr. Owl, your fire feels so-o-o warm.

Wind: Sw-i-sh! Sw-i-sh! I love this pla-c-c-e.

Snow: I'm going to enjoy my stay in your warm house. Where will I sleep?

Wind: Wheee-ee! I want to play a game with you, Snow. Let's blow out Mr. Owl's fire.

Mr. Owl: Oh, no! Don't blow out my fire. If you do that it will be as cold in here as it is outside.

Snow: Wheee! See me spread my white blanket of snow all over your cozy furniture.

Mr. Owl: Snow! Wind! You are my guests! This is no way to behave. Be good and sit by the fire.

Wind: Snow, I'm too warm now. Let's get cold again.

Snow: I'll cover the windows with icy designs—sw-i-s-h—and freeze Mr. Owl's pea soup into hard green ice.

68

Owl at Home Script *(cont.)*

Wind: I'll puff up and blow Mr. Owl's things all around his house. (*Blowing and swooshing sounds.*)

Snow: I can do better than that! I'll cover everything in here with snow, snow, snow!

Mr. Owl: Stop it! Stop it! I can't take any more. You two must leave at once!

Wind: But you invited us in. You can't chase away your guests.

Mr. Owl: Oh, yes I can! I asked you into my house, but not to have you ruin it. You must leave right now!

Narrator: Mr. Owl runs to the front door and opens it. (*An opening-door sound.*) Snow and Wind rush outside and Mr. Owl slams the door quickly. He gives a sigh of relief.

Mr. Owl: Good-bye!

Narrator: Mr. Owl is tired. He needs to take a nap. He sits in his soft chair.

Mr. Owl: I've learned my lesson. Wind and Snow do not belong in a house. I'll never invite them into my house again.

Narrator: Mr. Owl drinks a fresh cup of hot soup. He then takes a nap. As for Wind and Snow, they will have to stay outside—as cold as ever.

Wind and Snow: Mr. Owl is warm at last,
Safe from our windy and snowy blast.
Enjoying his soup and taking a nap,
Snuggled up in his warm winter cap.

Classroom Preparations

Bulletin Board Display

Create a bulletin board that will display your children's work. Begin by placing black bulletin board paper onto your display area. Cut a yellow circle "moon" out of construction paper; attach it to the top left corner. Add white cutout letters to spell your chosen title, such as "Who-o-o's the best at learning? Yo-o-u are!" Have the children make Hooty Owls (page 71) and add them to the bulletin board display. (The name of each child may be printed on the front of his or her Hooty Owl.) As the children complete art or written activities, display their work beside their owls.

Owls Learning Center

For success in your Owls Learning Center, be certain you. . .

- attractively decorate the center so your children will be motivated to spend time there working on new or reviewed skills.
- develop learning activities for all styles of learners.
- create language activities such as story starter ideas (page 24), drama activities (pages 57–62 and 65–69), and poetry (pages 23 and 57).
- add facts about owls (pages 76 and 77) and display the owl charts (pages 72–75).
- provide materials such as owl books (see pages 79 and 80), pencils, paper, art supplies, and game materials needed to complete the activities.

Hooty Owl

Materials
- 8 ½" x 11" (22 cm x 28 cm) sheets of tagboard
- bottle caps (the old-fashioned kind)
- dark-colored buttons (must be smaller than the inside of the bottle cap)
- transparent tape
- 2" x 4" (5 cm x 10 cm) pieces of yellow cellophane retangles
- scissors or craft knife

Preparation
Reproduce the Hooty Owl Pattern (page 71) onto tagboard, one per child. Cut out the eyes of the owls with scissors or a craft knife; discard the cutout circles.

Directions

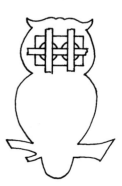

1. Color the owl and branch; cut them out.
2. Place the owl facedown on a flat surface. Lay cellophane rectangles over the two eye openings; tape the edges of cellophane to the tagboard.
3. Place a button in the center of each cellophane eye. Place a bottle cap over each button; tape each bottle cap securely to the back of the owl (as shown on the right).
4. Turn the owl over and watch the eyes move as you shake it gently.

Classroom Preparations *(cont.)*

Hooty Owl Pattern

Cut Out

Cut Out

Owl Reference Charts

Species	Habitat	Nesting	Foods	Range
Barn **Size:** 14–20 in. 37–51 cm	open fields and grasslands	dark and sheltered barns, old buildings, and hollow trees	small rodents, mice, moles, or badgers	areas near the Canadian-United States border
Screech **Size:** 7–10 in. 18–25 cm	open woodlands and areas of towns where large clusters of trees can be found	natural or woodpecker-made holes in trees, nest boxes, and chimneys	birds, insects, fish, small mammals, earthworms, and frogs	Southwestern Canada and most of the United States
Great Horned **Size:** 20–28 in. 51–71 cm	deciduous (seasonal leaves) and coniferous (evergreens) forested regions	old nests of hawks, magpies, or crows	wide variety of birds and ducks, small mammals such as house cats, small dogs, and mice	British Columbia and Washington state, some prairie areas and Western Plains region of the United States
Snowy **Size:** 14–17 in. 36–43 cm	open fields or tundra in North America	small holes in the ground	small birds, rodents, lemmings, fish, and insects	Arctic tundra, but have been found as far south as the Canadian-United States border

72

Owl Reference Charts *(cont.)*

Species	Habitat	Nesting	Foods	Range
Burrowing **Size:** 5–11 in. 13–28 cm	dry, open grassland and desert areas	abandoned ground burrows dug by marmots, prairie dogs, or woodchucks	insects and small animals such as mice, moles, voles, and squirrels	Southwestern Canada and Central/ Northwest United States
Spotted **Size:** 16–19 in. 41–48 cm	dense coniferous and old-growth forests	tree holes or cliff crevices	rats, mice, squirrels, bats, or other small mammals	Southwestern Canada and Northwestern part of Washington
Great Grey **Size:** 25–33 in. 64–84 cm	northern mountainous areas, dense forests	abandoned hawks' or crows' nests	small mammals and birds (**Note:** hunts during the day)	interior of Northern Canada
Elf **Size:** 5–6 in. 13–15 cm	desert cactus forests or dry grassy lowlands or savannas	giant saguaro cacti	insects, crickets, grasshoppers, caterpillars, and other small insects	Southwestern United States

Food Chain Chart

Plants depend on owls and other animals for nutrients from their droppings to survive and grow.

Owls depend on frogs or other small animals for food to survive.

Grasshoppers and other insects depend on plants for food to survive.

Frogs and other small animals depend on the grasshopper or other insects for food to survive.

Parts of an Owl

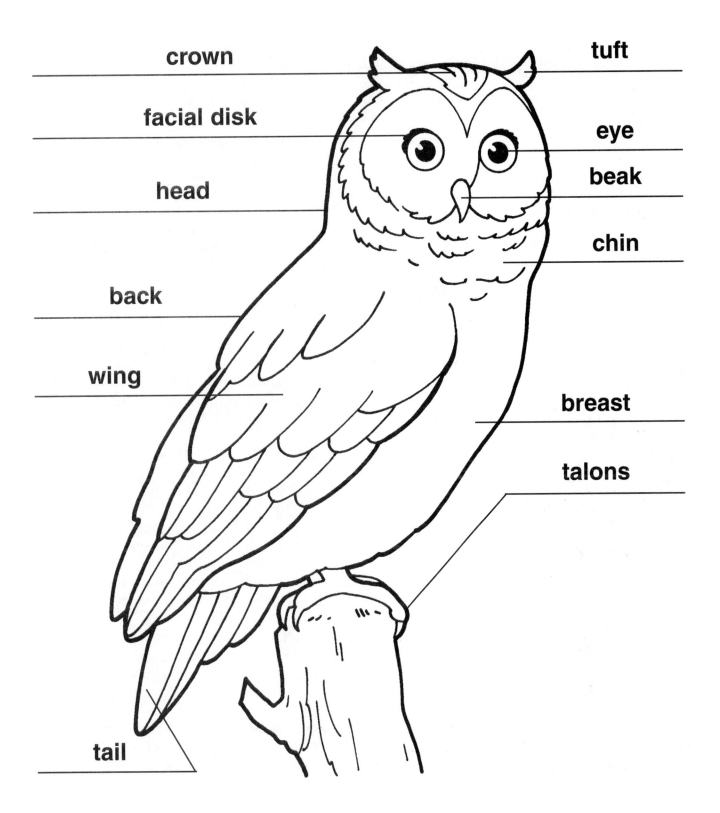

crown

tuft

facial disk

eye

beak

head

chin

back

wing

breast

talons

tail

Facts About Owls

Owls are impressive birds of prey with massive wings, piercing eyes, sharp claws, and strong talons. Owls are solitary creatures that display solemn and often times, frightening appearances. They have been part of an image of noble power and stature for many centuries. There are approximately 133 species of owls located throughout the world except in Antarctica and a few isolated islands.

Contrary to popular belief, not all owls are nocturnal (hunt only at night). About 80 owl species hunt at night, and the rest are crepuscular (active at dusk and dawn). The list below indicates the hunting habits of some of the well-known species of owls listed on the reference charts (pages 72 and 73).

Nocturnal	Crepuscular
Burrowing owl	Barn owl
Elf owl	Spotted owl
Great Horned owl	Screech owl
Snowy owl	
Great Grey owl	

Types of Owls: Owls are divided into two families—barn owls and typical owls. There are 10 species of barn owls. *Barn owls* are characterized by their heart-shaped facial disk which has earned them the nickname "monkey-faced owls." They have amusing actions, small eyes, long legs, are completely feathered, and have a serrated comb (a hard, flexible material) on the claws of their middle toes. Barn owls make the more traditional "hooting" owl sound. *Typical owls* are distinguished by their large eyes. Another important characteristic of typical owls is their peculiar call which sounds like wailing, screaming, or a barking dog.

Characteristics: Easily recognizable, owls are chunky birds with large broad heads and tufts of feathers around their eyes. The ear tufts are not actually ears at all. Owls' ears are small hole openings hidden behind their facial disks. Owls' feathers are soft and fluffy, which often make them seem larger and fuller than they really are. Most owls' plumage is patterned gray, brown, black, and/or white to help them blend in with their surroundings. Female owls are usually larger than the males.

Eyes: An owl has large, immovable eyes located on its facial disk. The eyes are fixed forward, and an owl usually watches objects with both eyes at the same time. It can judge distances well due to its binocular vision. Binocular vision means "a three-dimensional visual field." An owl's eye pupils can open or close to increase or decrease the amount of light let in. Its eyes focus easiest on noncolor tones. Since an owl cannot roll or move its eyeballs in its sockets, it has to literally turn its head to follow an animal; therefore, its neck is very flexible. An owl's eyelids close downward to shield its eyes from foreign matter.

Talons: An owl's talons have powerful razor-sharp claws to use as weapons and to help catch its prey. The talon has four clawed toes that are used to hook its prey and grasp it firmly. When an owl attacks, its toes are held in a stretched-out position. An owl also has one flexible toe that allows it to hold more securely onto its perch or hold on firmly to its prey.

Endangered Owls

To enjoy the many birds and animals of nature, we must work to protect their habitats. In spite of the work of professional environmentalists, there are many endangered bird species, and the number continues to rise. Scientists predict that there are several hundred animals on the world's endangered list today.

Species have vanished or become endangered for several reasons. The three main reasons are overkill for food, fur, or sport. Another significant reason is that the environments animals live in have been destroyed or changed. When a forest is cut down, hundreds of animals must find new homes. Likewise, when a swamp is drained for urban development, we take away the animals' habitats. When too many animals of a certain species are killed, another species is now without food and the food chain is disrupted. The owls' food chains have been disrupted, especially due to the destruction of forests and land areas.

The future of owls is largely dependent on the protection generated by concerned citizens. Encourage your children to become concerned about building safe havens for owls, birds, and other animals. A field trip to a local bird sanctuary or wetland area or a quiet walk in the forest will assist your children in becoming knowledgeable and understanding the part they can play in wildlife protection. If you cannot go on an outing, check your local community services to see if any environmental organization sends out representatives to inform the community. It so, have them come to your class for a presentation.

The Burrowing owls are in real danger. Their habitats are in the grasslands and deserts of North, Central, and South America. They build their nests in holes or burrows left empty by prairie dogs or marmots. The reasons for their decline has been largely due to farmers plowing the land and ruining the owls' nests. Also, farmers poison the owls' food source (insects and mice) by using pesticide sprays. In spite of all the efforts by biologists and environmentalists, fewer and fewer Burrowing owls are nesting.

The Spotted owl is in danger in the Pacific Northwest of the United States and along the Canada-United States border. These owls particularly like to inhabit dense, evergreen forest areas with tall trees and great undergrowth. The old-growth forests are being destroyed at an alarming rate by the logging industry. As the forests disappear, so do the habitat areas of the Spotted owl. In some areas entire forests have been cleared, which has threatening the owls' survival due to the disappearance of their food supply—rodents, bats, and other small mammals. Environmentalists have been trying to convince the loggers that the forests need to be selectively cut to permit the Spotted owl to retain its habitat. Because its environment is diminishing so rapidly, this shy owl is rarely seen.

Invitation and Award

A Hoot of a Time!

**You are invited to
an owling. . .**

When: _____

Where: _____

Who-o-o: _____

Who-o-o thinks you're the best?

I do-o-o!

To: _____

From: _____

For: _____

Bibliography

Fiction

Brown, Margaret Wise. *The Important Book.* Harper and Row, 1949.

Bunting, Eve. *The Man Who Could Call Down Owls.* Collier-Macmillan, 1984.

Collins, David R. *The Wisest Answer.* Milliken, 1987.

George, C. George. *There's an Owl in the Shower.* HarperCollins, 1995.

Green, Alain. *Ollie the Owl.* Children's Press, 1987.

Hamberger, John. *A Sleepless Day.* Scholastic, 1973.

Harris, Nicholas. *Owlbert.* Gareth Stevens Children's Books, 1989.

Hutchins, Pat. *Good-Night Owl!* Aladdin Books, 1990.

Lear, Edward. *The Owl and the Pussycat.* Scholastic, 1984.

Livingston, Myra C. *If the Owl Calls Again.* Collier, 1990.

Lobel, Arnold. *Owl at Home.* Scholastic, 1975.

London, Jonathan. *The Owl Who Became the Moon.* Dutton Children's Books, 1993.

Mahy, Margaret. *Feeling Funny.* Children's Press, 1993.

Mowat, Farley. *Owls in the Family.* Little Brown Press, 1961.

Norman, Howard A. *The Owl-Scatterer.* Atlantic Monthly Press, 1989.

Rice, Elizabeth. *Who-oo-oo.* Steck-Vaughn, 1990.

Taylor, C. J. *How We Saw the World.* Tundra Books, 1993.

Thaler, Mike. *Owly.* Harper & Row Inc., 1982.

Thompson, Richard. *Who.* Orca Publishers, 1993.

Yolen, Jane. *Owl Moon.* Scholastic, 1987.

Nonfiction

Arnosky, Jim. *All About Owls.* Scholastic, 1995.

Burton, Jane. *Benjamin and the Barn Owl.* Pan Macmillan Children's Books, 1992.

Burton, Jane. *Buffy the Barn Owl.* Gareth Stevens Children's Books, 1993.

Cameron, Angus. *The Nightwatches.* Four Winds Press, 1990.

Kappeler, Markus. *Owls.* Gareth Stevens Children's Books, 1991.

Ling, Mary. *Owl Magazine.* Scholastic, 1992.

McKeever, Katherine. *A Place for Owls.* Greey de Pencier, 1987.

Nero, Robert W. *Owls in North America.* Hyperion Press Ltd., 1987.

Stone, Lynn M. *Owls.* Rourke Enterprises, 1989.

Toops, Connie M. *Discovering Owls.* Whitecap Books, 1990.

Audio-Visual Materials

Sony Music Entertainment, Inc. *Forest Animals.* Music Entertainment, 1994.

Saintsing, David. *The World of Owls.* Oxford Scientific Films. Gareth Stevens Publishers, 1988.

National Geographic, Inc. *The Owl That Couldn't Give a Hoot.* National Geographic, Inc. 1989.

Web Sites

Basic Information on the Burrowing Owl
http://www.utep.edu

Jennifer's Owl Page
http://oz.uc.edu

Screech Owl Information
http://www.ntcnet.com

General Owl Information
http://www.acorn.group.com

Resource

Owl Pellets
Pellets, Inc.
P.O. Box 5484
Bellingham, WA 98227-5484
(360) 773-3012
Fax (360) 738-3402
A catalog is available upon request.

Answer Key

Pages 10 and 11: Sentence Strips sequential order

1. Late one winter night, Pa and I went out owling.
2. Pa and I silently as we walked into the woods.
3. Our feet crunched on the crisp snow as we walked into the woods.
4. Pa called to the Great Horned owl.
5. We went deeper into the dark woods.
6. We stopped at a clearing deep in the dark woods.
7. An echo could be heard coming through the trees when Pa called.
8. A Great Horned owl was landing on a branch.
9. The owl flew quietly back into the woods.
10. Pa said, "It's time to go home."

Page 30: Lunch with Owly

1. mice
2. fish
3. frogs
4. worms
5. lemmings
6. birds
7. bats
8. insects
9. grasshoppers
10. snakes
11. squirrels

Page 31: Owl Crossword

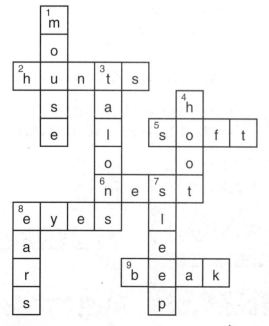

Page 32: Owly's Word Search

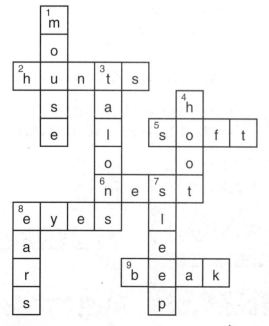

Page 35: Matching

1. Burrowing Owl—lives in burrows underground
2. Snowy Owl—feasts on lemmings
3. Barn Owl—has a heart-shaped head
4. Great Horned Owl—has large feathery tufts on its head
5. Screech Owl—makes a shrill whistle sound
6. Spotted Owl—lives in old-growth forest
7. Elf Owl—lives in a Saguaro cactus
8. Great Grey Owl—largest owl in North America

Page 49: Spotty Owl's Problem Solving

1. $4 + 2 + 3 = 9$ insects
2. $5 + 4 = 9$ trees
3. $3 + 4 = 7$ hikers
4. $4 - 3 = 1$ mouse
5. $4 - 3 = 1$ owl
6. $3 + 3 + 3 = 9$ animals